Jan Kachelmaier

Autonomous Vehicles in Germany

An Exploration of the Technology, Legal and Regulatory Environment, and Customer Readiness

Bibliografische Information der Deutschen Nationalbibliothek:

Die Deutsche Nationalbibliothek verzeichnet diese Publikation in der Deutschen Nationalbibliografie; detaillierte bibliografische Daten sind im Internet über http://dnb.d-nb.de abrufbar.

Impressum:

Copyright © ScienceFactory 2018

Ein Imprint der Open Publishing GmbH, München

Druck und Bindung: Books on Demand GmbH, Norderstedt, Germany

Covergestaltung: Open Publishing GmbH

Table of Contents

Abstract 5

List of Abbreviations 6

List of Figures 7

List of Tables 8

1 Introduction 9

2 Literature Review 12
    2.1 The History and Development of the German Automobile Industry 12
    2.2 Autonomous Driving 15

3 Research Aims and Contribution 27
    3.1 Research Aim 27
    3.2 Significance of the Study 27
    3.3 Research Question and Objectives 28

4 Methodology 29
    4.1 Research Design 29
    4.2 Data Collection 36
    4.3 Sampling Strategy 36
    4.4 Data Analysis 37

5 Primary Research Analysis 39
    5.1 Qualitative Analysis 39
    5.2 Quantitative Analysis 46

6 Discussion 59
    6.1 Technology 59
    6.2 Legal and Regulatory Environment 61

6.3 Customer Readiness 64

6.4 Key Recommendation for German OEMs 66

7 Guidance for Future Research **68**

7.1 Theoretical and Methodological Limitations 68

7.2 Suggestions for Future Research 69

7.3 Personal Reflection of the Paper 70

References **72**

Appendices **88**

Appendix A: VW vs. main Competitors: Units Sold in 2004 and 2014 88

Appendix B: SAE International Levels of Autonomous Driving 89

Appendix C: GM Leads, Tesla & Apple Trail Deeply In Navigant Research Self-Driving Report 90

Appendix D: US States with Enacted Autonomous Vehicle Legislation 91

Appendix E: Rogers Product Adoption Curve 92

Appendix F: Survey on Customer Readiness 93

Appendix G: Age Distribution of Survey Respondents 97

Appendix H: T-test on Willingness to use AVs by Gender 98

Appendix I: ANOVA on Willingness to give up One's own Car and Importance of Driving Experience for Female Participants 99

Appendix J: T-test on Influence of Positive and Negative News of AVs on males 100

Abstract

The automobile industry is one of Germany's strongest and most important industries. However, the diesel emission scandal is a crack in the perceived quality, reliability and the overall premium image of Germany. The automotive industry is facing its greatest and most critical change since the invention of the automobile. Four megatrends (connected, autonomous, shared and electric) are dominating the 21st Century and the entire automotive industry around the world. Various companies are working intensively on the development of the next major milestone in human history that incorporate all megatrends, autonomous vehicles. The technology is perceived to be disruptive and thus many challenges and obstacles remain before the new technology becomes superior to human drivers.

This research paper aims to explore and investigate the status quo of the development of autonomous vehicles at German OEMs. It further aims to identify future impediments until market entrance and recommend managerial actions. The paper focuses on three key pillars: Technology, legal and regulatory environment, and customer readiness which are indispensable for a successful implementation of autonomous vehicles. Various interviews are conducted with experts from OEMs and automobile associations and potential German end-users are surveyed. The analysis revealed various insights which are discussed and recommendations for German OEMs are given.

List of Abbreviations

AD	Autonomous Driving
ADC	Autonomous-Driving-Car
ADS	Autonomous-Driving-Shuttle
AV	Autonomous Vehicle
BMW	Bayerische Motoren Werke
DV	Depending Variable
FCA	Fiat Chrysler Automobiles
GM	General Motors
GPS	Global Positioning System
ICE	Internal Combustion Engine
INS	Inertial Navigation System
IT	Information Technology
IV	Independent Variable
Lidar	Light Detection and Ranging
NHTSA	National Highway Traffic Safety Administration
ODD	Operational Design Domain
OEM	Original Equipment Manufacturer
Radar	Radio Detection and Ranging
R&D	Research and Development
SRS	Simple Random Sampling
TCO	Total Cost of Ownership
TCU	Total Cost of Usage
UN ECE	United Nation Economic Commission for Europe
VC	Vienna Convention
VW	Volkswagen
V2I	Vehicle to Infrastructure
V2V	Vehicle to Vehicle

List of Figures

Figure 1. Production of Passenger Vehicles by Country from 1961-2015 13

Figure 2. Car Brand Map based on Cost and Product Excellence 14

Figure 3. Levels of Autonomous Driving. Adapted from SAE J3016 16

Figure 4. Types of Regulation for Automated Driving 21

Figure 5. Research Onion 29

Figure 6. Willingness to use AVs. 47

Figure 7. Willingness to give up one's own Car. 48

Figure 8. Willingness to give up one's own Car by Gender. 48

Figure 9. Evaluation of Daily Mobility Factors. 50

Figure 10. Preferred Shape of AV and Concerns of Riding in an AV without Self-Steering Possibilities. 51

Figure 11. Safety Considerations of AVs. 52

Figure 12. Trustworthiness of AV Providers. 52

Figure 13. Fear of Cyberattacks on AVs. 53

Figure 14. Influence of Positive and Negative News on Males. 53

Figure 15. Influence of Positive and Negative News on Females. 54

Figure 16. Knowledge of AVs by Gender. 57

Figure 17. Key Recommendation for German OEMs. 67

List of Tables

Table 1: TCA Steps. 38

Table 2: TCA Identified Themes - Technology. 39

Table 3: TCA Identified Themes - Legal and Regulatory Environment. 43

Table 4: Chi-Square-Test of Gender and Willingness to give up one's own Car. 49

Table 5: Anova on Willingness to give up one's own Car and Importance of Driving Experience for Male Participants. 49

Table 6: T-test on Influence of Positive and Negative News of AVs on Gender. 55

Table 7: T-test on the Influence of Positive and Negative News of AVs on Females. 56

Table 8: Difference in Knowledge of AVs by Gender. 58

1 Introduction

With a turnover of around 404 billion Euro which account for approximately 20% of the total German industry revenue, the automobile industry is one of Germany's greatest and most important industries (GTAI, 2017). The great success of the German automobile industry evolved over decades and ensured Germany a place at the top of the world's carmakers. However, with the diesel emission scandal, the industry and OEMs took loses, especially VW (Volkswagen). The VW's stock price plunged by more than 50% within a few months (La Monica, 2015). The scandal is a crack in the perceived quality, reliability and the overall premium image of cars made in Germany (McGuinness, 2015). The timing of the scandal is rather unfortunate since the automotive industry is facing the greatest change of all time. Four megatrends are dominating the 21st Century and the entire automotive industry around the world. The tremendous and disruptive[1] trends and its emerging technologies[2] are affecting and changing the industry completely (Heineke, Möller, Padhi, & Tschiesner, 2017; Morgan Standley, 2016). The first megatrend is shared. Similar to other industries, the sharing economy influences the automotive industry as car and ride sharing players entered the market (Grosse-Ophoff, Hausler, Heineke, & Möller, 2017). The second megatrend is electric. Global warming, the tightened $Co2$ reduction targets and the pioneering of Tesla lead to a drastic increase in electric vehicles. The adoption of electric vehicles is ongoing as carmakers around the world are electrifying their vehicles (Times, 2017). Connected is considered to be the third megatrend of the automotive industry. As the digitalization process of the society proceeds, it vastly affects automobiles with respect to internal and external connectivity for optimizing vehicle operation and maintenance as well as for passenger's utilization of travelling time (McKinsey, 2014). Though autonomous is considered to be the fourth megatrends, it is also perceived as the ultimate combination of all megatrends. As a matter of fact, the emerging technology is seen by Germany's transport minister Alexander Dobrindt as the 'greatest mobility revolution since the invention of the car' (BMVI, 2016). The reason is that AVs (autonomous vehicles) are utilized in

---

[1] A disruptive technology is defined to be an innovation that replaces existing technologies and are causing significant shifts in business and social environments (Christensen, 2013).
[2] An emerging technology is a term that is relatively defined as a new technology that is currently being developed (Congress of the United States Office of Technology Assessment, 1995).

shared manners, are electrified and connected to the environment. The technology is perceived as the solution to the market movements and answer to the megatrends in the automotive industry. The reason is that AVs have the potential to reduce the Co2 emission and eliminate a significant portion of traffic jams while increasing mobility and space utilization in urban areas (Kuper, 2016).

While these megatrends appose threats to some, Dr. Dieter Zetsche (CEO of Daimler AG) conceives the transformation differently as he believes that 'changes are not a threat, but an opportunity' (VDA, 2017). Nevertheless, the changing environment levels the playing field to some extent which increases the number of competitors as newcomers[3] are entering the automotive industry. This impacts the global competition and increases the pressure on German OEMs (original equipment manufacturers) to innovate. But not only vehicles are affected, rather the entire ecosystem of mobility has to be adopted and change in order to enable a successful implementation of AVs (Wladawsky-Berger, 2016). Consequently, the infrastructure must be adjusted simultaneously to the development of AVs. This requires a co-working and cooperation between political and economic forces. Moreover, cooperating is vital in order to stem the significant burden of the transformation as well as to ensure and maintain the top level position of the German automobile industry on a macroeconomic perspective. Otherwise, competitors from the USA and China might take over the German market and harm one of Germany's most critical industries (McKinsey, 2016).

This research paper is guided by the following structure: The paper starts with a literature review including the three research pillars of AD (autonomous driving): Technology, legal and regulatory environment, and customer readiness. The chapter is followed by a description of the research aim and contribution which contains the defined research question and objectives. The methodological research design, data collection, and data analysis approach is elaborated within the methodology section. Afterward, the conducted primary research is analysed based on the characteristics of the collected data (qualitative and quantitative). In the following chapter, the key summarized findings are discussed regarding their theoretical as well as managerial implications and aggregated recommendations for German OEMs are given. The paper ends with an elaboration of the theoretical

---

[3] Within this paper the term or phrase newcomers includes tech firms such as Waymo and Apple that are aiming to enter the automotive industry.

and methodological limitations of the research project and gives an aggregated prospect for future research.

2 Literature Review

2.1 The History and Development of the German Automobile Industry

The history of the automobile industry can be divided into the following five stages or phases: Firstly, the initial automobile development, secondly the development of the modern automobile, thirdly the pre-World War II-phase, fourthly the post-World War II-phase and fifthly the phase of the 21st century.

The early roots of the automobile can be found in the very beginning of the history, around 100 C.E when the Greek philosopher Heron of Alexander used steam to resolve a ball on an axle (Collier, 2006). Various engineers from different countries developed interim stages of a fully functioning and usable automobile (Weeks, 2011). The ultimate breakthrough in the development was made in Germany by Carl Benz as well as Gottlieb Daimler in 1885 (Weeks, 2010). The two engineers developed the first modern automobiles which used an Otto cycle engine (Sinclair, 2004). Carl Benz's engine was attached to a three-wheeled vehicle while Gottlieb Daimler used a two-wheeled bicycle (McNeese, 2000). During the 1890s many other engineers started building modern automobiles such as the German OEM Opel in 1899 (Pohl & Rudolph, 1990). The industry started to grow very slowly as only a few duplicates were made (Flink, 1990). At that time, French car manufacturers led the way in terms of production (McNeese, 2000). Due to the costly production process and the materials, the price of the products was high and industry growth was limited (Mullin, 2010). The next major capstone in the history of the automobile was achieved by the American Henry Ford who founded the Ford Motor Company in 1903 and introduced the assembly line to the automobile production in 1913 (Banham, 2002).

During the beginning of the 20th century, the early growth phase of the automobile industry, many new and today's leading car manufacturers entered the industry. The American OEM GM (General Motors) was founded in 1908 (Fourie, 2016) which acquired Opel during the end of the 1920s (Kudo, Kipping, & Schröter, 2004). Shortly after, the German OEMs Audi (1909) and BMW (Bayerische Motoren Werke) followed in 1916 (Joseph, 2013). In 1931 Porsche was founded (Joseph, 2013) and in 1937 VW (Parment, 2014) as well as Toyota entered the industry (Fujimoto, 1999). Before World War II, engineers made significant improvements with respect to the technical abilities and applications of the vehicles. Shortly before and during the beginning of World War II, the number of vehicles produced increased, mainly due to military reasons (Lepage, 2007). The real production boom occurred after World War II during the major reconstruction phase in Germany between 1954 and 1965. During this period, local production and export increased significantly to 52% in 1965, while imports were relatively low at about 10-12% (IFO Institute for Economic Research & Shuka Institute of Research, 1997). The production in Germany further increased in the following years, though with a weaker slope, while the Japanese kept rocketing to the top, as illustrated in Figure 1 (U.S. Department of Transportation, n.d.).

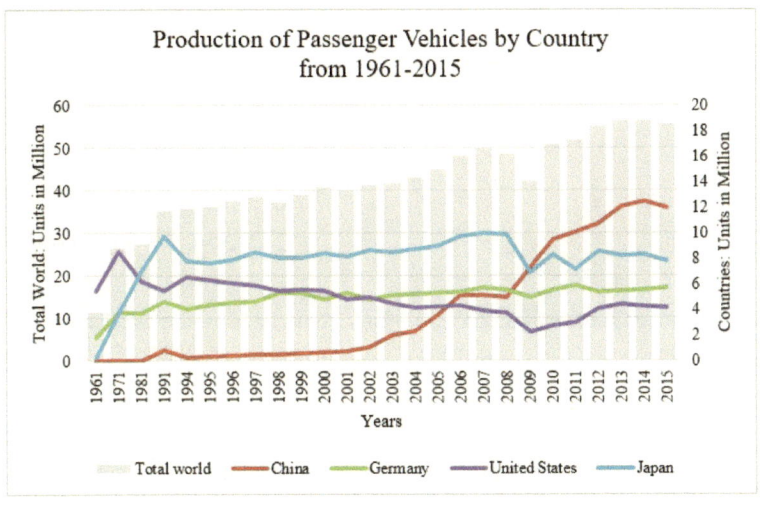

Figure 1. Production of Passenger Vehicles by Country from 1961-2015

In accordance with Table 1-23: World Motor Vehicle Production, Selected Countries (Thousands of vehicles), by U.S. Department of Transportation, n.d., Retrieved July 16, 2017, from Bureau of Transportation Statistics:
https://www.rita.dot.gov/bts/sites/rita.dot.gov.bts/files/ publications/national_trans.

While the US car industry started struggling, German OEMs benefited from an unexpected growth due to the opening up of East Germany and the Eastern European market (Preissl & Solimene, 2003). Besides, German OEMs kept widening their portfolio through acquisitions as well as the development of new models (Parissien, 2013). From early on and until the end of the 20th century, the 'Made in Germany' stamp and the internationally associated quality with the mark, lead to a position at the top of the premium passenger vehicle market (Joseph, 2013). At the beginning of the 21st century, all German brands were positioned at the top of each segment as illustrated by Figure 2 (Hirsh, Hedlund, & Schweizer, 2003). While the brand VW operated at the top of the mass-market segment and Audi positioned itself between the premium and luxury segment, BMW, and Mercedes as well as Porsche were already perceived as the top-notch of the premium or luxury segment.

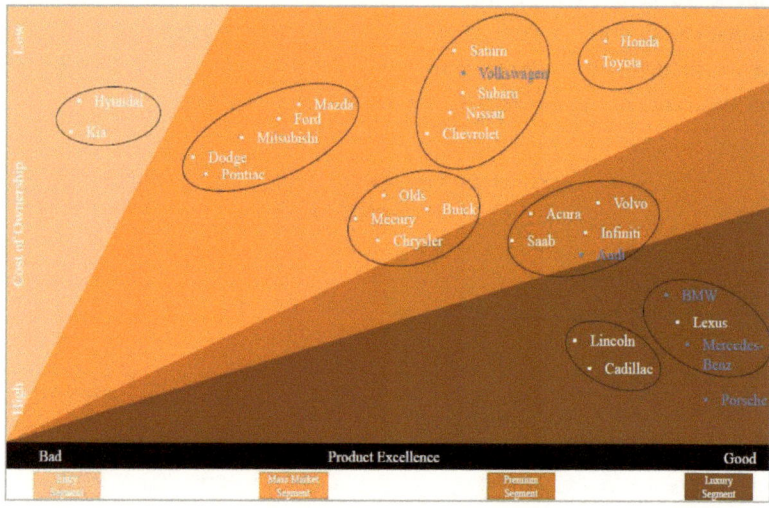

Figure 2. Car Brand Map based on Cost and Product Excellence

Adopted from Reality Is Perception: The Truth about Car Brands, by E. Hirsh, S. Hedlung & M. Schweizer, 2003, Retrieved July 16, 2017, from Strategy + Business: https://www.strategy-business.com/article/03302?gko=fbb50.

Nevertheless, German OEMs were hit hard by the financial crisis in 2008 (Boston, 2008), but the industry was able to recover faster than expected (Kollewe, 2012). By the end of 2014, VW was at the top of the global automotive industry (see Appendix A). By then the company had recovered from the financial crisis and build a significant portfolio of different automobile brands. Besides already holding several commercial vehicle brands and sub-companies, in 1988 and 1999 VW acquired three top passenger luxury brands: Bugatti, Lamborghini, and Bentley (Roberts, 2005). The OEM SEAT was already part of the portfolio since 1986 and in 1991 Skoda joined the group (English, 2011). A few years later in 2012, Porsche was also acquired (Topham, 2012). Mercedes and BMW widened their portfolio as well with respect to passenger and commercial vehicles (Freyssenet, 2009). By 2015, two third of the total production from German OEMs was made outside of Germany, indicating the continuation of outsourcing low-value assembly processes (VDA, 2016).

The diesel scandal in 2015 (Taylor & Potter, 2017) as well as the increasing performance of Tesla and the technological trends changed the environment of the German automobile industry significantly (Heneric, Licht, & Sofka, 2005). Today, the industry is subject to the dynamic megatrends of connected, autonomous, shared and electric (Daimler AG, n.d). As a result of the dynamic trends, VW and Mercedes changed their corporate strategy, moving from an automobile manufacturer towards a mobility provider (McKinsey, 2016). While electric vehicles, connectivity features and shared services are already available or entering the market within the next couple of years, AD is considered to be the next major milestone in the automotive industry that will influence everyone and change the world (Alexander, 2013).

2.2 Autonomous Driving

2.2.1 The history and development of autonomous driving

The first significant step in the history of AD is dated back to the 1930s and 1940s when the idea of an automated highway system was proposed (Meyer & Beiker, 2014). During the second half of the 20th century, more American researchers and developers became active and concentrated on the field of an automated highway driving. In Germany, it was Mercedes Benz which reached a milestone during the 1980s as the first automobile manufacturer to test AD on streets in Bavaria, though without any traffic at that time (Siciliano & Khatib, 2016). At the beginning of the 21st century, the research filed was expanded and AVs started to be the main focus of manufacturers and researchers (Meyer & Beiker, 2014).

Though AD is considered to be a disruptive technology, the development and implementation process are rather continuous. While the NHTSA (2013) defined only five phases or four AD-levels, SAE International (2014) extended the definition. Figure 3 illustrates the six phases or five AD-levels ranging from no automation to full automation. The phases or AD-levels can be divided into two main parts (SAE International, 2014): In the first part, the human driver monitors the driving environment (up to AD-level 2) and in the second part, the automated driving system monitors the driving environment (from AD-level 2 until AD-level 5).

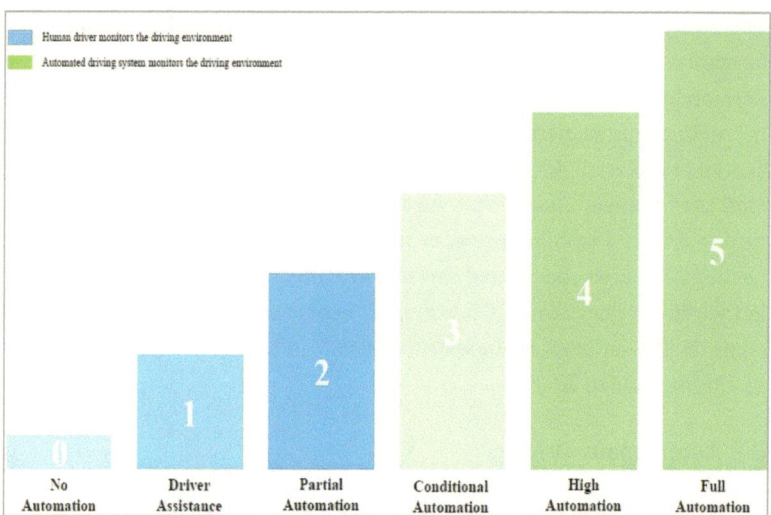

Figure 3. Levels of Autonomous Driving. Adapted from SAE J3016

Taxonomy and Definitions for Terms Related to Driving Automation Systems for On-Road Motor Vehicles by SAE Internal, 2014: SAE International.

The first two AD-levels are already existing and AD-level 3 will be reached between 2018 and 2020 (Roland Berger, 2014). The first production of AD-level 3 vehicles has already started as Audi revealed its new A8 which demonstrates its intelligence and self-driving applications with Audi's new traffic jam pilot (Taylor, 2017). The first AVs with AD-level 4 are estimated to be leaving the factories between 2020 and 2025 (Roland Berger, 2014). Whereas, AD-level 5 is seen as a future prospect as it requires AVs to be not limited to any driving mode that a human drier can manage which includes aspects such as no limitation by speed or driving environment (see Appendix B)[4].

Various different OEMs as well as newcomers are developing the system behind AVs. Though Hanley (2018) considers certain companies to be leading in developing AVs (see Appendix C), the overall competition is still ongoing. While Tesla, VW, Apple, and Toyota are developing the technology on their own, others formed strategic alliances and cooperations such as GM and Lyft, Volvo and Autoliv, Daimler and Bosch, BMW and Intel (including Mobileye) and Waymo with FCA (Fiat

---

[4] Since AD-level 5 is perceived as a long term future prospect, in the following the single term AV refers to AD-level 4 vehicles.

Chrysler Automobiles) (CB Insights, 2017). The partnership of Waymo and FCA is limited to a certain number of vehicles. Therefore, Waymo aimed but failed so far to recruit Ford as a vehicle supplier (Carty, 2017). Ford on the other hand is now using the resources of Lyft (Isaac, 2017).

The technology of AVs, including specially designed AVs and conventional vehicles with AD-ability[5], offers many benefits with respect to the commercial as well as private transportation of passengers and goods (Ozimek, 2014; Omohundro, 2014). Firstly, the number of accidents could be reduced significantly, as about 90% of all car accidents are caused by a human error. Secondly, time and efficiency could be increased drastically, as traffic jams could be reduced since fewer vehicles are needed due to attractive ride sharing and the increased utility of each shared AV. Furthermore, congestion could be diminished because AVs are able to drive in packs and do not take wrong turns. As a result of the increasing efficiency, consumption as well as pollution and carbon emissions are reduced, especially because AVs are powered by electricity. As a consequence of the gained efficiency, commuting and travelling time in general as well as the associated cost could decrease (Bunghez, 2015). Therefore, the consumers in the taxi and logistic industry could benefit from faster and cheaper deliveries (Mark, 2017; DHL, 2014). Disabled and handicapped people could gain mobility because driving a car would not be necessary for high mobility standards anymore. Thirdly, the technology could have positive implications on the infrastructure. The parking situation could be de-escaladed as no permanent parking spot inside urban areas would be needed. The size of car lanes could be reduced since AVs make no steering mistakes and thus less room for steering adjustments is required. Fourthly, the tedium as well as the stress of commutes could diminish due to the fact that passengers are able to utilize their time differently (Kuper, 2016).

2.2.2 Status quo of autonomous driving in the German automobile industry

The following three paragraphs display a secondary literature review of the three research pillars: Firstly, the technology, secondly the legal and regulatory environment and thirdly the customer readiness.

---

[5] The term specially designed AV refers to a vehicle that is developed for AD by purpose, while the term conventional vehicle with AD-ability refers to a traditional vehicle that is upgraded with AD-abilities.

Technology. The emerging technology offers various promising advantages and benefits, though several R&D (research and development) obstacle remain before implementing the technology becomes possible. The technological development challenges are similar for all OEMs around the world as most components are developed nonexclusively by top-tier suppliers. One exception is the 'brain' of the vehicle, the AI (artificial intelligence) which interprets the driving environment and steers the vehicle. The key development areas can be divided into the following three categories: Sensing and interpreting the driving environment, communication and cybersecurity (Anderson, et al., 2016).

Sensing and interpreting the driving environment. Anderson, et al. (2016) define a three-phase sense-plan-act design that AVs underline. Firstly, the driving environment is sensed. Secondly, the vehicle's action is planned and eventually carried out through an actionable command in the third step. These loops occur all the time and in parallel. Cameras and various sensors are responsible for scanning the environment and gathering input information. The difficulty for the sensors is to accurately perceive the driving environment as it is a very dynamic and complex situation. Especially sensing the variety of different elements is a challenge such as various road obstacles including pedestrians, wildlife, debris, cyclists or traffic events such as roadwork, congestion or crashes as well infrastructure conditions including various and rough surfaces, poorly marked roads or lanes, detours and defect traffic lights. The lidar (light detection and ranging) system is able to determine obstacles by using laser ranger finders. However, it functions reliably only over shorter ranges and on certain well reflecting materials. Whereas the Velodyne system works to a range of up to 120 meters. But, on low reflecting materials such as asphalt, the system only works up to 50 meters. On small distances, infrared systems are capable of detecting lane markings without lighting. Another sensor technology used in AVs is radar (radio detection and ranging) which works well on metallic objects such as vehicles but poorly on non-metallic obstacles such as pedestrians. Therefore, pedestrians and bicycles can be spotted by infrared sensors. Ultrasonic sensors are accurate on short ranges of 1 to 10 meters and thus are very useful for parking assistance and backup warning. In general, each sensor provides a different kind of data and therefore has other benefits and limitations. Due to that reason, AVs usually use a combination of sensor systems in order to offset the limitations. For example, sensor suits are used to perfectly localize a vehicle. It is a combination of GPS (global positioning system) and INS (inertial navigation system). Even under ideal conditions, the GPS system is often inaccurate by several meters. This error increases drastically when obstacles or terrain occlude the sky such as in urban areas. Therefore, the system is coupled with the INS. The greatest challenge is the drift that occurs when the system relies only on the INS system as GPS is unavailable. As a result, many AVs draw on prebuild maps, but the difficulty with prebuild maps is the construction and maintenance of an accurate map. Since AVs underlie tight financial constraints, integrating adjustable, multifunctioning sensors is uneconomically. OEMs have to choose between different sensors and consequently between various capabilities and limitations at different price points in order to fulfil their customer's needs. Another key technical challenge is the accurate functionality under extreme environmental circumstances. The accuracy of sensors declines dramatically during serve precipitation, heavy snow, extreme temperatures or dense fog. Different terrains pose challenges as well as sensors are rather made for one terrain or another. For example, sensors might have issues either on a flat environment or steep hills. The different materials of the road such as asphalt or dirt require different abilities of the sensors due to varying reflection of materials (Attias, 2017). Apart from environmental challenges, sensor failure is another key difficulty since safety is of utmost importance. Sensors may fail due to physical damage, age or electrical reasons (Ploeg, 2017). Therefore, an internal sensing system and algorithm that can detect components that are not performing adequately is required. More precisely, an ultra-reliable simple low-level system with basic sensor functions is needed that takes over in the event of degradation or failure. The system has to detect and override control rapidly in order to be able to steer the vehicle away from dangerous areas such as high traffic roads or blind curves (Anderson, et al., 2016).

Interpreting the driving environment is the second step. After the sensors delivered the input information and data, the 'brain' of the vehicle analyses the information and plans the action as well as eventually carries it out. With perfect perception, computers are extremely accurate and reliable. However, they lag humans especially when it comes to interpreting the driving environment. The interpretation is done by the 'brain' or AI of the vehicle. AI comprises of machine learning and deep learning which are two different approaches of analysing and processing input data (Pathak, 2017). Deep learning is applied by many top-notch high tech companies such as Drive.ai, AImotive, and FiveAI. While it works exceptionally well in most situations the major drawback is the impossibility of understanding a decision of the AI. The decision process is a 'black box' embodied by neural networks consisting of millions of nodes that analyse raw data and make decisions. Due to the limitation of understanding the decision process, some developers such as Ford rather focus on machine learning which is grounded on algorithms and logic (Toews, 2017). The underlying algorithms in this approach are not as sophisticated as human brains or neural networks yet. Thus, they are more vulnerable to difficult environmental conditions which impose great interpretation challenges. The algorithms allow to comprehend and re-enact the machine's decision and thus problems can be explicitly addressed. Another key challenge of AVs is the decision in an ethical dilemma situation such as the trolley problem in which the AV has to choose between the life of humans (Overly, 2017). Daimler takes a leading position in this dilemma, as the OEM announced to priorities its passengers and not pedestrians based on the reason that AVs should primarily save those that the AV has direct control over (Morris, 2016).

Secondly, vehicle communication. This includes HMI (Human Machine Interface), the communication of the vehicle with humans, as well as communication of V2V (vehicle-to-vehicle) and V2I (vehicle-to-infrastructure). Communicating is essential for informing humans and for ensuring a smooth traffic flow as it allows AVs to coordinate actions, especially when crossing large intersections or making a turn onto a fast-moving road (Savic, Schiller, & Papatriantafilou, 2017). The communication between the vehicles could relive the sensors in some tasks and thus solve some technical challenges such as recognizing black ice, other hazardous conditions or crashes. To enable the communication, various federally funded research programs aim to develop standards for DSRC (dedicated short-range communication) (United States Department of Transportation, n.d.). The decisive challenges to overcome are the creation, maintenance, and insurability of an ultrareliable public infrastructure. An adequate V2V communication system requires the deployment of high-level communication technology as well as communication standards and platforms. Additionally, the localization of each AV has to improve and be extremely accurate (Anderson, et al., 2016).

Thirdly, cybersecurity. Cybersecurity is a key issue because AVs heavily rely on electronic systems and thus require much higher security standards and virus detection systems to ensure functionality and passenger's safety. Due to the strong dependency on software and thus software updates, the concern of cyberattacks is high (Driscoll, Roy, Ponchak, & Downey, 2017). Assuring software quality and reliability is an increasing challenge as AVs need to connect and perform tasks on diverse platforms. A simple software update requires access to the internet which may enable computers to attack vehicles with viruses. Also due to the connection to other vehicles, infrastructure, and the internet, AVs are more vulnerable to cyberattacks. Software and hardware of AVs need to be also locked up from users in order to prevent 'jail breaking' attempts. Overall, it is unalterable that cybersecurity standards of AVs are put on another level for all system in an AV as one small hacked system such as the tire pressure monitor may provide access to the entire vehicle due to the connection of the systems. A possible solution could lie in the emerging technology of blockchain as it could allow an efficient validation of transmitted information (Bordonali, Ferraresi, & Richter, 2017).

Legal and regulatory environment. Another key success factor of AVs is an adequate and corresponding legal and regulatory environment (Anderson, et al., 2016). Overall, the key concerns or challenges to be addressed are general regulatory aspects of AD and insurance or product liability regulations. A sound and modernized legal framework is necessary to enable the realization of AVs. Since the governmental dependency on the automotive industry is high, the adoption of the regulatory framework could bring many benefits from a macro perspective. Moreover, non-binding enactments and rules can be used to create a sustainable regulatory environment. Figure 4 illustrates various tools separated by the time horizon (ex ante – forward looking and ex post – backward looking) and the actor (public and private) (International Transport Forum, 2015).

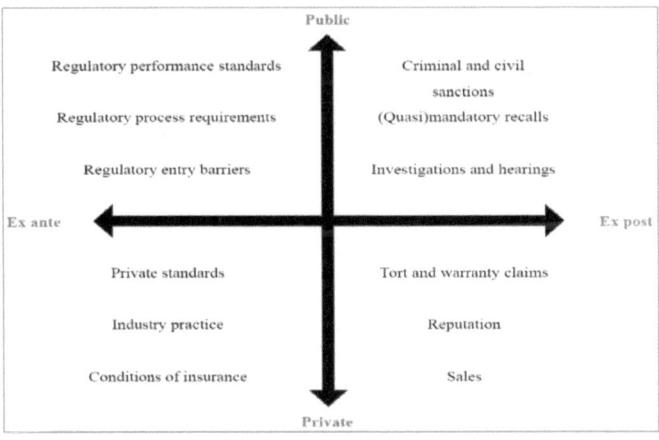

Figure 4. Types of Regulation for Automated Driving

Adapted from Automated and Autonomous Driving: Regulation under Uncertainty by the International Transport Forum, 2015. Retrieved from https://www.itf-oecd.org/sites/default/files/docs/15cpb_autonomousdriving.pdf.

The primary consideration and decision to make is to determine whether AVs should be treated specially or generally with respect to regulations. This means, that either new and standalone rules as well as agencies regulate AVs or current slightly adopted rules are in place and ordinary agencies are responsible. The next key consideration is to decide whether policy or technology should lead. This has significant implications on the uniformity or flexibility of AV regulations. While proactive policies can create legal clarity that supports investment and deployment decisions, unsuitable or unrealistic laws and regulations can freeze the development and reduce the flexibility. Due to the advantages and disadvantages, informal dialogues can be a beneficial solution in order to provide and form legal certainty for investment decisions while remaining flexible and adaptable. A further decision has to be made concerning ethical issues and the product liability and responsibility. The obligations and liabilities of owners and operators as well as OEMs have to be clarified (International Transport Forum, 2015).

In Germany, AVs are mainly treated generally and not specially, thus, the Road Traffic Regime is responsible. The German Road Traffic Regime is based on the German national law which is influenced by European and international law. In general, the technological development is much further advanced than the regulatory framework. Consequently, various non-national laws and regulations impose challenges and contradictions to the utilisation of automated functions such as the VC (Vienna Convention) or UN ECE (United Nations Economic Commission for Europe) regulations. The VC defined in Article 8(1) that a driver must be a person. In 2016, the VC was adopted and partly refers now to the UN ECE regulations. This simplifies and increases the adaptability of the legal and regulatory environment as changing only the corresponding UN ECE regulations in the future is sufficient (Norton Rose Fulbright, 2016). AD-level 2 functions such as the lane keeping and changing assistant, adaptive cruise control or parking assist bear no legal risk anymore and are already implemented in various vehicles (Roland Berger, 2014). Though, limitations remain, for example for the lane keeping and lane changing assistant. The UN ECE Regulation No. 79 allows a short period steering assistance by the vehicle before the driver has to take over again. The lane changing assistant has to be initiated by the driver via the direction indicator in order to comply with the UN ECE Regulation No.48 (Norton Rose Fulbright, 2016). Laws for AD-level 3 are installed since 2017. As a result, specific driverless functions such as an autonomous parking system on private areas are usable and will be implemented in future vehicles (Norton Rose Fulbright, 2017). The German legislation enabled road-testing for AD-level 4. This allows the driver to take the hands of the wheel and eyes of the road while the vehicle steers and breaks autonomously. In case of an accident, the driver is held responsible if the accident occurs under his watch, while the manufacturer takes responsibility when the self-driving system is in charge and the vehicle crashes due to a system failure. The law is to be reviewed in two years. Then, adjustments will be made to keep up with to the technological development and clarification regarding the data protection as well as data collection will be attempted (Wacket, Escritt, & Davis, 2017). Since testing AVs is indispensable for the future success, two critical German automobile clusters installed further testing infrastructure. Firstly, digitalization processes of the A9 motorway in Bavaria is proceeding. Secondly, test beds in cities and highways are planned including an inner-city section in Ingolstadt and a combination of motorways, highways and inner-city areas in Baden-Wuerttemberg (Norton Rose Fulbright, 2016; Daimler, 2017).

Ethical implications of AVs are not only a development consideration of OEMs but also a governmental decision. The German Federal Minister of Transport and Digital Infrastructure published a list of 20 ethical rules for the guidance of automated and connected driving. The guidelines are clear regarding a possible collision with animals or property, as humans' lives have priority. However, the trolley problem is considered as unsolvable. Thus, the guidelines require AVs to avoid such situations in the first place. Primarily due to the reason that these complex situations cannot be standardized or programmed to replace the judgement of a responsible driver. (Federal Minister of Transport and Digital Infrastructure, 2017).

Product liability and insurance policies impose another barrier for AD (BBC, 2015). The current liability regime consists of three pillars, the driver, the keeper (owner) and the manufacturer which includes suppliers. The current German Road Traffic Act, sec. 7 states that the owner of a vehicle may be held liable for any damages caused by the vehicle, regardless of any fault since the owner bears all the risk of operation. On the other hand, according to the paragraph 18 of the German Road Traffic Act, the driver is generally responsible unless it is proven that he did not negligently cause any damages (Norton Rose Fulbright, 2016). Whereas the OEM is considered to be liable whenever a product defect occurs regardless of any negligent behaviour. While the German Product Liability Act is not very comprehensive, the liability based on the general tort law is more extensive. This law requires proof of the negligence of the OEM or the suppliers. In general, the owner and the OEM are joint debtors, thus the plaintiff may request compensation from either. Even though both are may be held reliable, one or the other may claim resource from the joint debtor due to the actual reason for the accident. In case of a technical failure, the owner or practically the insurer of the owner may request resources from the OEM or the supplier. Since AVs are likely to reduce the number of human failures, accidents caused by technical issues may become the primary reason for accidents and thus the liability shifts to the OEM. Therefore, attempts are being made to hold the OEM reliable for any damages occurred in order to simplify and clarify the liability issue. While most OEMs omit a clear commitment, Volvo decided to announce that it will take full responsibility for all technical defects, but not for accidents caused due to inappropriate use of the customer (BBC, 2015). In the US, the legal and regulatory environment for AVs is more advanced with respect to certain aspects. Up to 2017, legislations or executive orders related to AVs were passed within 26 states (see Appendix D). The state of Nevada requires a certificate of compliance which must be issued for an AV by the manufacturer or a licenced AV certification facility. The certification comes with additional cost and the compliance with several technical specifications (Anderson, et al., 2016). The major weakness in the USA is the absence of a federal law and thus the difference between the state laws. The variance imposes potential challenges and obstacles. Firstly, users might have issues when an AV is intended to operate in several states. Secondly, manufacturers face difficulties in complying with every AV law within the USA. In order to increase the deployment of AVs, the government aims to impose the first major federal legislation within 2018 which would regulate the safety requirements of AVs. As the legislation becomes effective, OEMs would be required to build AVs that are equally safe or safer than current vehicles. But, OEMs would not be penalized for missing the safety requirements in the first year (Shepardson, 2017).

Customer readiness. In order to create a successful product, the market side and the customer demand is indispensable. By 2035 more than 12 million AVs are expected to be sold per year on a global scale. This results in a market capture of around 25% of the vehicle market (Mosquet, et al., 2015). To achieve this, the population needs to be ready and accept the emerging technology. Due to the initial high price of specially designed AVs, the customers of OEMs are estimated to be on the one hand almost exclusively taxi companies and on the other hand their subsidiary mobility providers, in case OEMs are repositioning themselves in the supply chain such as VW and Daimler. In the B2B market, customer readiness depends on rational and economic arguments. Whereas in the B2C market the success of AVs depends various considerations of end-users. The step from a conventional vehicle without driver assistant function to a specially designed AV or a conventional vehicle with AD-ability is significant. Thus, incremental steps in the development of driver assistant systems and AD-levels are critical for the technology acceptance (Lipson & Kurman, 2016). As every innovation, AVs are subject to the adoption curve (see Appendix E) and in the early phase, only innovators are expected to use specially designed AVs and buy conventional vehicles with AD-ability (Rogers, 2010). Over time, more people adapt to the new technology for various reasons. The most rational reason is the decrease in cost. While in the beginning mostly companies are expected to operate specially designed AVs in a B2C sharing model due to the high costs, this is expected to change over the lifecycle of the technology and C2C (customer to customer) specially designed AV sharing could increase (Janasz, 2016). The pace and the range of adoption is difficult to predict. For example, the transition from horses to motor vehicles lasted several years. According to Chief Economist for the Consumer Technology Association Shawn DuBravac the noticeable transition might take another 20 to 25 years. The duration of transition depends on various factors. According to Lang, et al. (2016) technology acceptance and customer readiness imposed a major obstacle in the past but this is likely to vanish over time as experience and familiarity of AVs increase. Lang, et al. (2016) conducted a survey that indicates significant customer readiness of AVs in India and China (only 5% and 8% respectively where unwilling to take a ride in an AV) whereas in the US, UK and Germany the rates of unwillingness were significantly higher at 30%, 31% and 36% respectively. Nevertheless, different surveys investigating the customer readiness regarding technology acceptance, displayed significant variations in the findings depending on the formulation of the questions (Putre, 2016). This indicates the indecision of the population regarding the technology and the associated benefits and threats. While people acknowledge the benefits on the one hand, on the other hand people are being strongly influenced by the risk and unknown of the technology (Regan, Horberry, & Stevens, 2014; Jahankhani, et al., 2017). Overall, six key concerns that are holding back the acceptance of AVs can be identified. Firstly, uncertain reliability which is associated with the increased responsibility of the technology and a corresponding, potentially higher rate of failure. Secondly, safety concerns including harm caused by computational (AI) failure or programmed damage reducing accidents (ethical dilemma) as well as cyberattacks. Thirdly, giving up control and putting the personal welfare in the responsibility of a machine is a major concern. Similar issues can be found in the aerospace industry, as people are more worried about taking a plane than driving their car, regardless of their statistically increased safety (Peterson, 2016). Fourthly, AVs are confronted by scepticism as the technology is rather unknown, which in general is a typical issue of emerging technologies and new products (Friar & Balachandra, 2016). Fifthly, the lost freedom that people associate with the ability to drive instantly when and where they want (Peterson, 2016). Sixthly, many people associate fun with driving a car and thus they are not willing to give this up. However, the fun of driving a car substantially depends on the driving environment, as driving during traffic jams or in crowded urban areas is rather stressful (Lang, et al., 2016).

3 Research Aims and Contribution

3.1 Research Aim

This research paper aims to explore and investigate the status quo of the development of AVs at German OEMs. It further aims to identify future impediments until market entrance and recommend managerial actions. Due to the paper's requirements including the limited time scope, the research project is considered to be cross-sectional in nature. This means, that it concentrates on a specific point in time and changes over a long period are not observed as it is in longitudinal research projects (Saunders, Lewis, & Thornhill, 2012). Furthermore, the paper focuses and thus primary research is conducted in the following three key pillars that are indispensable for a successful implementation of AVs: Technology, legal and regulatory environment and customer readiness.

3.2 Significance of the Study

The automobile industry is one of Germany's strongest and most important industries (Lewis & Zitzlsperger, 2016). It is also one of the largest employers in Germany as around 800.000 people are directly and one out of seven jobs are indirectly linked to this industry (Bargende, Reuss, & Wiedemann, 2017; Smale, 2015). At this time the automobile industry is at its greatest and most critical change since the invention of the automobile (Maxton & Wormald, 2004). Traditional OEMs are changing their strategy and are now aiming to become mobility provider (Isaac & Boudette, 2016). This change requires different key skills and core competitive advantages since the primary essence of an AV is no longer the vehicle's hardware but the software. Therefore, skills in the field of IT (information technology) are required as artificial intelligence and machine learning are the key cornerstones of AVs (Foster, Ghani, Jarmin, Kreuter, & Lane, 2017). The industrialization of AVs is a top strategic priority of German OEMs for several reasons. Firstly, OEMs are not seeking a cost but technology leadership. Hence, OEMs are mostly operating at the top of the premium passenger vehicle segment and technology advancement is a core competitive advantage. But the danger of losing the superior market position and becoming a first-tier supplier of the automobile industry is at a high-level (Abuelsamid, 2017). Apart from the market position, many OEMs have invested a significant amount of money in the development of the technology while expecting higher returns. Overall, their existence is at stake, especially if OEMs fail to commercialize the technology (The Economist, 2017).

Besides, the government is also very interested in a successful implementation of the technology due to the importance of the industry to the German economy as well as the technology's benefits for the end-users. The advantages of the technology are very appealing to Germany since the government has to react to the tightened CO_2 regulations, the related emission debate regarding diesel engines and ICEs (internal combustion engine) in general, and to reduce the increasing issues of urban density and traffic jams (Arthur D. Little, 2009). But the customer readiness with respect to the technology is unclear, especially because many people still believe AVs to be a part of the far future (Rosenzweig & Bartl, 2015).

In summary, industrializing AVs is essential for the survival and the market position of German OEMs. It is also critical for the German government in order to ensure employment, maintain tax incomes, reduce emission, and offset the effects of urban density. However, many obstacles and unanswered questions are yet to be resolved and addressed to enable the implementation of the emerging technology. This research project supports and enhances the development by further investigating in this domain, identifying challenges, and proposing managerial actions.

3.3 Research Question and Objectives

Based on the purpose of this research project, the following overall research question is formulated and investigated:

What is the development status and what are the impending obstacles of AVs in Germany?

In order to uncover the formulated research question accordingly, the following three research objectives are addressed:

Objective 1

Explore the current technological development of AVs at German automobile manufacturers and identify possible future obstacles.

Objective 2

Establish the current legal and regulatory environment regarding AVs in Germany and investigate the potential future development.

Objective 3

Investigate the current customer readiness and technology acceptance of future private end-user in the German market.

4 Methodology

4.1 Research Design

4.1.1 Empirical strategy

A rigorous methodological approach is essential when it comes to researching and investigating a futuristic and complex topic such as AD with the aim of obtaining valid findings (Laws, Harper, & Marcus, 2003). Saunders et al. (2012) developed a research onion which serves as a general framework to guide the methodological reasoning underlying this research (see Figure 5).

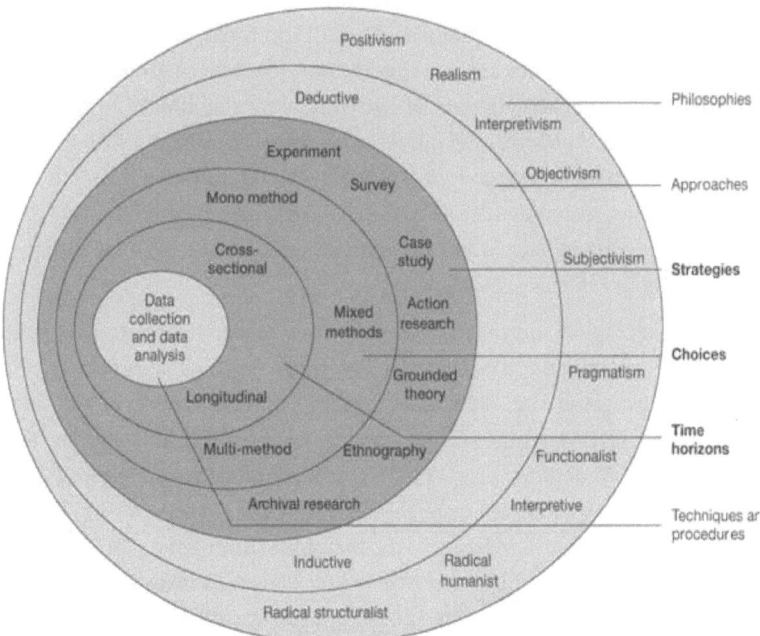

Figure 5. Research Onion

Adapted from Research Methods for Business Students, by M. Saunders, P. Lewis & A. Thornhill, 2012, Essex: Pearson Education.

The research onion illustrates different research philosophies which are not superior to another but rather serve different aims and are thus more appropriate for specific research topics and aims. Based on the aim of the project and the research question, pragmatism is considered the most appropriate research philosophy. This philosophy guides the research methodology in a practical and flexible manner which allows addressing the key research problem in the most beneficial way (Klenke, 2016).

This research paper is based on a deductive approach as it is grounded on the research findings of other scholars (Crowther & Lancaster, 2008). In general, two rigours can be identified which apply to the choice of the research methodology (Smith & Dainty, 1991). The two major methodologies are qualitative and quantitative research (Quinlan, 2011). The first rigour, qualitative research, emphasizes and focuses on the generation of non-numerical data (Punch, 2016). Qualitative research is an useable and valuable tool for investigating and analysing either specific areas that require expert knowledge or abstract issues that are hard to be grasped quantitatively (Saunders et al., 2012). In these cases, conducting qualitative research in any form such as expert interviews, focus groups or surveys with open-ended questions is beneficial (Denzin & Lincoln, 2000). On the other hand, the second rigour includes the quantitative research with the core focus on gathering numerical data (Balnaves & Caputi, 2001). Quantitative research is predominantly applied within deductive research approaches (Quinlan, 2011). Due to the nature of numerical data or information, surveys are the most frequently utilized tool (Dahlberg & McCaig, 2010).

The methodological approach chosen for this research project was guided and influenced by previous researchers and their research approaches: McKinsey (2016) investigated the development of the current trends in the automotive industry by interviewing various experts from OEMs, associations and other stakeholders. Anderson, et al. (2016) applied qualitative research in form of experts interviews to investigate the technological aspects of AVs. Furthermore, for researching legal barriers of AD, the association ENO (2013) also applied qualitative research by means of expert interviews. To investigate in the opinion of the customer, Abraham, et al. (2016) applied quantitative research in form of an online-questionnaire when analyzing the customer's trust in AVs and its features. Abdu-Dalbouh (2013) researched the technology acceptance by customers and Schoettle and Sivak (2014) investigated in the public opinion of AVs by using an online questionnaire.

Due to the aim and nature of the research project, a concurrent mixed method approach is chosen. This approach enables the exploitation of the advantages of research tools and the investigation in the three key research areas through the most suitable population (experts and potential customers) by means of quantitative and qualitative research.

Qualitative research is applied to the first two key research areas (technology as well as legal and regulatory environment). This research method is essential since extensive knowledge in the two research fields is required in order to obtain valuable and precise information (Bogner, Littig, & Menz, 2009). Moreover, qualitative research enables an accurate utilization of open-ended questions. This allows to validate or reject findings from secondary research as well as to explore the experts' knowledge related to the research area in-depth (Flick, 2014). While qualitative research can be carried out in various forms, Saunders et al. (2012) suggest focus groups or interviews in form of one-on-one interviews with experts in order to gain useful and profound insights. The predominant use of focus groups is for the investigation in a group consensus regarding a particular topic through a communicative discussion (Liamputtong, 2011). Whereas one-on-one expert interviews aim to elicit particular information from individual experts with no influence of another person during the interview (Halperin & Heath, 2017). Consequently, the most appropriate method for this project is considered to be one-on-one expert interviews as the objective is to interview various experts separately in order to find consensus or discrepancies in the different statements and beliefs regarding AVs. One-on-one expert interviews can be conducted in three different ways: structured, semi-structured or unstructured (Jawadekar, 2011). Structured interviews follow a pre-determined script of typically closed-questions and are strictly directed by the interviewer, thus the interviews are inflexible since deviations are not permitted (Beidel, Frueh, & Hersen, 2014). Whereas unstructured interviews follow a not pre-determined script. The interviews are rather an open conversation that is not guided or bounded by any constraints which allow discussing any topic in any way (Meyer & Booker, 2001). The downside to this interview approach is that it also reduces the efficiency of the interview and the aim might be missed as the conversation is not driven by a specific guideline (Wilson & Sharples, 2015). Due to the limitations of structured and unstructured interviews, semi-structured interviews are most frequently applied by researchers (Mayoh, 1991). Semi-structured interviews combine the utilization of a rigid structure to ensure a fluid conversation while maintaining flexibility with respect to the evolvement of the interview (Lewis-Beck, Bryman, & Liao, 2004). These benefits are embodied by the mixture of pre-determined open-ended and closed questions which allow the interviewer to explore topics in depth and breath (Tryfonas, 2016). Though both types of research questions can be used, predominately open-ended questions are employed (Wengraf, 2001). In general, no minimum or maximum number of minutes exist for expert interviews, the length of the interviews is rather determined and influenced by various factors such as scope and topic of the research project as well as the availability of the interviewed experts (Awad & Ghaziri, 2007). Due to the constraints of time and scope of the project as well as the availability of the experts, the ideal duration is considered to be 15 to 30 minutes.

The third key research area, customer readiness, is investigated through quantitative research. Quantitative research consists of three major types: descriptive, correlational and experimental (Goodwin & Goodwin, 1996). A descriptive quantitative research method is the choice for this domain as it is considered to be the most appropriate method, because further exploratory and in-depth information are not the objectives of this paper. Additionally, the descriptive method requires less time and resources (Salkind, 2010). A questionnaire instead of standard interviews is utilized in order to explore the macro and common consensus of future private end-users and not the in-depth opinion of a few individuals (Finkbeiner, 2017). Questionnaires can be conducted in various ways such as in-person, via telephone or online (Oakshott, 2012). In-person questionnaire, followed by telephone-questionnaires, yield the highest response rate, but these methods are also much more time consuming and require more resources than online-questionnaires (Fielding, Lee, & Blank, 2008). Online-questionnaires are especially handy when it comes to research on a large scale. (Abbott & McKinney, 2013). Consequently, an online-questionnaire is considered to be most appropriate and is chosen for this research. The questionnaire is designed to exclusively consist of closed questions in order to simplify the data analysis and to avoid high rates of nonresponse and break-off. The online-questionnaire should take no longer than 5 to 10 minutes, as recommended by fellow researchers (Czaja & Blair, 2005). The finally selected questions of the survey are in line with the research methodology and derived from the secondary research.

4.1.2 Research timeline

The research timeline is created in accordance with the FMP framework, provided by the program for the Master in International Business at the Grenoble Ecole de Management. The created research timeline consists of 14 milestones. The key milestones are the submission of the FMP title on the 30th of September 2017.

The methodology and research aims which are completed on the 23rd of October 2017. On the 27th of October 2017, the process of conducting secondary research is finished. Based on the findings of the literature review, the specific research aims as well as the research question are formulated. Afterward, primary research is conducted in form of expert interviews and an online questionnaire. Due to the availability of the interview partners, the phase of primary research is finished on the 2nd of February 2018. The analysis of the primary research data is conducted in parallel part by part once the corresponding data is collected and finalized on the 28th of February 2018. The following days and weeks are used to write the discussion, finalize the content of the project as well as to review the created work. On the 11th of March 2018, the audit in form of two peer reviews is submitted and minor adjustments and corrections are made in the following weeks. Eventually, the FMP is submitted on the 14th of April 2018.

4.1.3 Primary research respondents and sample size

To gain a holistic view of the defined research problem, a triangulation of the sources is beneficial (Given, 2008). The pool of respondents in this research paper consists of experts in the field of AVs from OEMs and associations as well as of private future end-users.

The target respondents for the interviews are experts in the field of technological development and regulations with respect to AVs. The experts are either employed by German OEMs or are part of an automobile association. To ensure credible data, the experts are required to have worked for at least two years and acquired particular knowledge regarding the investigated fields of AVs (Katsirikou & Skiadas, 2012). The appropriate sample size for the qualitative research is considered to be five interviews, based on the aims and constraints of the project. Two interviews are conducted with OEMs in the area of technological development and another two in the legal and regulatory environment. The fifth interview partner is a major German automobile association which is interviewed regarding both the technological development and the legal and regulatory environment of AVs. Overall, the vast majority (four) of these interviews are conducted with experts from OEMs as direct information from the manufacturers is considered to be the key due to the currentness and scope of information. Nevertheless, bias has to be considered due to the strong link of the participants to the industry and thus the technology.

The target population for the quantitative primary research consists of future private German end-users who are currently at the age of 20 to 30 and are not working in the automobile industry. This specific target group is selected for the following reasons: Firstly, private future customers are chosen since the technology acceptance of entrepreneurs and corporations is primarily based on economic benefits. Once the technology offers a TCO (total cost of ownership) advantage, entrepreneurs and corporations are willing to adopt (Keay, 2011). Secondly, the specific age target is selected because once the technology is commercialized, the early primary customer target group consist of people at the age of 20 to 40 years as their adaptability to new a technology and changeability to established habits is the highest (McKinsey, 2016; Korosec, 2016). People under the current age of 20 years are not selected for the research project as their knowledge regarding AVs is deemed to be limited and thus inaccurate data could be the result (Hess, 1990). Thirdly, to minimize bias with respect to the generated data, neutral or non-pre-influenced potential future customers are selected. The participants are considered to be neutral or non-pre-influenced when they are not working in the automobile industry. Due to the reason that a correlation between people working in the automotive industry and their willingness and openness to adopt or switch to AVs is established (Zolait, 2013).

In general, the sample size (number of participants) in quantitative research should be five times higher than the number of questions in a questionnaire (Sreejesh, Mohapatra, & Anusree, 2014; Hair, Wolfinbarger, Money, Samouel, & Page, 2011). The conducted survey consists of 12 questions and thus a sample size of at least 60 people is selected for this research paper.

4.1.4 Ethics

Ethical conduct and data integrity are essential for the validation and credibility of this research paper (Blumberg, Cooper, & Schindler, 2014). Thus, this research project follows a rigorous ethical code of conduct including the following two aspects: Firstly, protection of anonymity and right to privacy. Secondly, informed consent.

Ensuring the participant's anonymity and protecting the right to privacy is indispensable for generating honest and thus realistic data. Therefore, the identity of all participants is confidential and is not made public at any time. The interviews are conducted in an environment that ensures privacy and integrity of all communicated information. The same applies to virtual interviews as several are conducted online via Skype or other telecommunication applications in order to be compatible with the individual time schedules of the interview partners.

Prior to starting the interview, participants are asked if the interview can be audio recorded, only in order to simplify the process of creating a word-by-word transcript of the interview. Participants are also informed regarding the process of creating the interview-transcript. After the creation, participants are given the chance to review the transcript, make adjustments and eventually sign the document. Any references to the participant's name or the name of the company are replaced by a participant number and a generic company name such as ABC Company. Nevertheless, the tutor as well as any GGSB staff may review the responses for validation and grading of this academic paper. Thereby, participants are ensured that the responses remain absolutely confidential and are not reviewed or accessed by any other. After the analysis is conducted and findings are drawn from the interviews, all participants are given the chance to review the work and express concerns or request changes if necessary. The changes are made according to the request in order to ensure accurate reflections of the interviewees' opinion and to ensure full anonymity of the participants and their corporations. This procedure is inevitable for achieving results of high quality since the interviews are part of the basic input and the primary source for the derived recommendations that are later on shared with a wider audience. During the entire quantitative research part, participants are assured of the confidentiality regarding their data. Since the questionnaire is conducted online, the participants' right to privacy is ensured by means of being able to take the questionnaire individually at a private place without any disturbance or influence of others.

Throughout the data collection process, the intentions of the research are fully disclosed to all participants, in advance to their consent of participating in this research project. All interview partners and participants of the online-questionnaire are briefed and informed with respect to the procedures guiding the collection, storage and access of the corresponding primary data. Participants of the interviews are contacted via email. The email contains a short and formal invitation and an explanation as well as a thorough participant information sheet. Participants of the online-questionnaire are also informed via an email regarding the research and ethics by a second participant information sheet. The invitation email is followed by an in-depth briefing on the first page of the online-questionnaire. Participants aren't deceived at any time.

4.2 Data Collection

4.2.1 Data collection tools

The data collection tools for the primary research vary with regard to qualitative and quantitative information. Qualitative data is retrieved from the conducted expert interviews through an audio recording and handwritten notes. After the interview, the information is manually converted into a written transcript, for the purpose of the qualitative analysis. On the other hand, quantitative data is extracted into an Excel-Sheet from the online platform GoogleForms where the questionnaire is conducted.

4.3 Sampling Strategy

The sampling strategy is a critical part of the methodology. A research project with a thorough sampling strategy can lead to up-to-date and low-biased data in an efficient way (Taylor, Sinha, & Ghoshal, 2006). Overall, collecting data from three different sources, OEMs, automobile associations, and customers enables a data triangulation and hence increases the credibility and validity of the findings (Given, 2008). The sampling strategy consists of two parts: The qualitative and the quantitative sampling strategy.

Interviewing all German car manufacturers and associations in-depth by conducting numerous interviews, is out of scope for this research project. Three different OEMs and one automobile association have been selected for this project based on various factors such as role and involvement in AD as well as position within the automotive industry. The actual interview partners within the organizations are selected based on a non-probability sampling strategy due to the purpose of the study and the fact that the entire population is unknown and cannot be individually identified (Konthari, 2004). Within the non-probability sampling strategy, a purposive approach in form of expert sampling is selected as it allows to adapt to the ability of the respondents regarding their knowledge and possible contribution to the study (Kumar, 2011). Factors such as gender, age or nationality are not considered. The person's expertise is the key priority in order to generate accurate and valid data. Therefore, only interview partners who have an extensive knowledge and expertise in the field of AD are selected (Katsirikou & Skiadas, 2012).

With respect to the consumer side, a probability sampling strategy is considered most appropriate in order to find representative and generalizable insights

(Marsden & Wright, 2010). Within the probability sampling strategy, a multistage sampling approach is deemed most suitable with respect to time, scope and cost (Pfeffermann & Rao, 2009). The multistage sampling approach consists of four steps: Selecting the target population, selecting the accessible population within the target population, building clusters and conducting a SRS (simple random sampling) for the final selection of the respondents (Martinez-Mesa, Gonzáles-Chica, Duquia, Donamigo, & Bastos, 2016). Since surveying the entire target population of Germans between 20 and 30 years is hard to realize, time consuming, and costly, an accessible while representative population within the target population is selected (Warner, 2013). The accessible target population is chosen and extracted by using a social networking site (Joosten, 2012). In the next step, all people are erased who do not fulfil the requirements of nationality, age and professional occupation (Ang, 2014). Afterward, all participants' names are replaced by a generic candidate number. The clusters are created based on gender (male or female), resulting in two different pools of 621 candidates, 247 females and 374 males. After the clustering, a SRS-approach is executed via Excel in order to select the final respondents within both clusters. The selected respondents are then contacted, briefed and invited to participate.

4.4 Data Analysis

The data analysis of the primary research is divided into two parts, the quantitative and qualitative analysis. The qualitative analysis follows the comprehensive TCA (thematic content analysis) (Kvale & Brinkmann, 2009). This analytical process includes seven steps as displayed in Table 1 (Mason, 2013):

TCA Steps	
1	Data transcription for the analysis
2	Familiarization and obtaining a general sense of the data
3	Coding by hand: Categorization and labelling of data
4	Identification of reoccurring themes

Methodology

5	Assessment of interrelation of themes and descriptions
6	Interpretation of meaning behind themes and descriptions
7	Checking validity and reliability

Table 1: TCA Steps.

Note. Adapted from Qualitative Researching, by J. Mason, 2013 by SAGE.

Firstly, the information from the interviews is transcribed. Secondly, a general familiarization and sense of the data is obtained. This means getting a broad view on the data and grasping different qualitative categories through reading and re-reading the transcripts. Thirdly, the labels and categories for the coding process are set in order to allow to get further and more specific insights from the qualitative data. Fourthly, the reoccurring themes are identified and marked within each transcript. Fifthly, the interrelation of themes and their description is analysed. Sixthly, the identified themes and their description are interpreted to extract the essence of the data. Seventhly, the findings are verified regarding validity and reliability in order to ensure high quality and accurate output.

The second part of the primary research analysis consists of the quantitative analysis of the conducted survey on customer readiness. Each part of the survey and the acquired data has an intrinsic value. Thus, the main challenge of the quantitative analysis is to analyse the data as well as to present the findings in the most insightful way, relating to the questions asked and the research objectives (Saunders, Lewis, & Thornhill, 2012). Microsoft Excel is chosen and used to extract the intrinsic value from the generated data as the tool is an efficient choice. The descriptive data analysis is utilized to display insightful aspects of the variables. By reviewing responses of future potential customers, the requirements and needs for AVs can be extracted. In addition, the value and importance of each criterion for the customer readiness can be revealed. This enables the analysis to provide a solid foundation and indication of the current customer readiness with respect to AVs.

5 Primary Research Analysis

5.1 Qualitative Analysis

The five conducted semi-structured interviews are analysed using the TCA approach. The interview transcripts are coded by hand and assigned to a superior category. Afterward, the codebook is created which summaries the previous findings and displays the nine reoccurring themes. The themes are separated and assigned according to the corresponding research pillar.

5.1.1 Technology

Overall, five themes are identified. The reoccurring themes are displayed in Table 2.

TCA Identified Themes – Technology	
Number of Themes	Technology
1	R&D
2	Market
3	Autonomous Vehicle
4	Business Model
5	Automobile Associations

Table 2: TCA Identified Themes - Technology.

The first theme, R&D, covers three key categories: R&D areas, R&D challenges, and status quo technology. Various experts consider the AD system including sensors and the highly correlated development of AI to be the critical research area of AVs. Communication to infrastructure can be considered as part of a sensor system (input information). Nevertheless, most experts believe that AVs need to be able to steer around in any environment without information from external sources. Cybersecurity is less seen as a challenging research area, but more as a standard or requirement which can and has to be fulfilled. Moreover, the interior layout including the user interface becomes more relevant. Within those research areas, several challenges remain. A key challenge is to improve sensors and to reduce the limitations. Areas for improvement include recognition of objectives and the abilities to operate in a challenging driving environment or under extreme weather conditions. Further, developing the abilities of AI is critical to enable a better analysis of the data. CPU capacity in the vehicles and the reliability of AI (deep learning approach) need to be increased while costs have to be decreased. In general, more complex and challenging deployment environments increase the requirements for sensors and AI as for example mountainous areas require greater AD skills than flat areas. The main challenge of communication is the limitation of range, latency, and availability, while for cybersecurity it is to ensure a most comprehensive cyber protection by creating a holistic security system. Most experts consider vehicles to be poorly protected against cyberattacks today and more sophisticated barriers are needed, but the ability to achieve full protection is doubtful. Not only OEMs are facing challenges in developing AVs, but newcomers such as Waymo are also confronted by certain difficulties. While special commercial AVs are already on the market such as in agriculture and forestry, some experts believe that much of Germany's AD technology is already developed but not on the market yet and not tested in unpublicized areas.

The second theme, market, contains five categories: Leading countries, leading companies, competition, AV deployment and market segmentation. The experts' opinions diverge with respect to the technological leading countries as some consider Germany to be the leader especially with respect to the sensor technology, while others see the USA in the lead. It is similar regarding the leading companies as no company has proven yet to build a functioning driverless concept in series and thus a clear leader cannot be identified. However, the expert's opinions indicate that the two German OEMs, Daimler and Audi, are deemed to be leaders of the industry. Great potential is seen in Waymo to become the single leader, whereas Tesla and BMW are perceived as less progressive. Considering AVs in form of ADSs (autonomous-driving-shuttles), leading firms are Easy Mile and Navya. Looking at the competitiveness from a country point of view Germany's strength is its technological development. While various technologies are widely used and already assembled in current AVs, others are yet to be made public. On the contrary, the USA's strengths are on the one hand especially the advanced AI systems and on the other hand firms such as Google or Microsoft that have tremendous advantages in integrating and connecting the living and working environment with AVs. On a company level, Audi's strengths are associated with the abilities to develop high-end technologies, similar to Daimler in cooperation with Bosch, which strengths are also the R&D know-how and the combined financial resources. On the contrary, even though Waymo realized the difficulty of developing AVs, the company has a significant advantage in testing AD. Combined with its advanced AI, the firm only has to find a large supplier of vehicle platforms in order to become the leading provider of AVs. The interviewed experts consider Uber to be less strong, especially with respect to the technological development, as it is not the company's core competence. Tesla's competitiveness is on a lower level as the competitors' sensor systems are more advanced. Since Apple has only announced to produce AVs but never shown any technological concepts the company's competitive edge is perceived as very low. Most experts consider traditional OEMs to be in an advantageous position due to their sensor system development. German OEMs in particular can exploit their competitive advantage of offering a hybrid of premium sport drive experience and autonomous comfort in traditional vehicles with AD-ability. Nevertheless, they need to be careful as their competitive edge on ICEs is dwindling since eDrive is pushing forward and the competition increases as various new competitors are entering the market of vehicle mobility. OEMs believe that a competitive advantage can be gained by focussing on the key attributes of AVs and developing a greater and more sophisticated concept than their competitors. Differentiation can be possible by quality, technology including the sensor system, an advantageous market position and involvement of customers as well as the integration of the living and working environment in AVs. Security and safety are rather seen as requirements that have to be fulfilled in the end. With respect to the deployment of AVs, experts believe that AVs are not able to operate 365 days per year by 2025. Besides, firstly specially designed AVs are considered to be introduced in urban and gated areas. ADSs can be an extension of the public transport, while conventional vehicles with AD-ability are deployed in intercity sections. Considering possible market segmentations, experts see much potential for niche markets within the AD segment. Different customer needs in urban and intercity areas enable a differentiation and possible separation factors can be price or type of AV (specially designed AV or conventional vehicles with AD-ability).

Autonomous vehicle is the third theme, which includes the categories AV attributes and AV specification. The attributes that an AV has to offer are use case specific and thus vary by geographic deployment as well as ownership since passengers have different needs. In general, AVs have to offer an appealing mobility package which includes a useful utilization of the travelling time, efficiency, convenience in various ways such as availability and proximate pick up locations, a smart integration into the mobility environment, an according way of driving, a strategy based premium or standard feeling while ensuring safety and security.

On the other hand, ADSs primarily need to provide user friendliness, efficiency in terms of cost reduction while also providing safety and security. Considering AV specifications, a distinction is made between conventional vehicles that offer manual as well as AD-abilities and specially designed vehicles which do not have any steering options. Experts believe that in the far future, the deployment of AVs in especially challenging environments such as mountainous areas can be enabled by theoretically equipping and adjusting or advancing the sensor system including the AI of AVs.

The fourth identified theme is the business model including business strategy and sales model. Most German OEMs are aiming to become a holistic mobility provider and by pursuing a two-way strategy with both AV types (conventional vehicles with AD-ability and specially designed AVs). Considering specially designed AVs, the differentiation between ADCs (autonomous-driving-cars) and ADSs has to be made. In contrary to German OEMs, newcomers usually do not want to build entire AVs, but rather purchase the vehicle and equip it with their AD technology. Their goal is to capitalize on their strengths such as their sophisticated mobility business models and great market capitalization while partnering up with vehicle providers (OEMs). Overall, a major part of the development and success of OEMs depends on top-tier suppliers as they develop various AD components. With respect to revenue streams, conventional vehicles with AD-ability will predominately be sold to end-users and specially designed AVs will be primarily acquired by specific operators such as robotaxi companies. In the luxury segment, revenue streams are unlikely to change as AVs will be sold to end-users, sharing models are relatively unattractive due to the characteristics of the segment.

The fifth theme, automobile associations includes the aim and purpose and responsibility of associations. Automobile associations are vital platforms which are used for discussion and collaboration of OEMs, suppliers and the government. The associations take care of general technological concerns and are responsible for negotiating widely accepted standards.

5.1.2 Legal and regulatory environment

In total, four reoccurring themes are identified and recognized in the TCA analysis as displayed in Table 3.

TCA Identified Themes - Legal and Regulatory Environment	
Number of Themes	Legal and Regulatory Environment
1	Legislations and Regulations
2	Ethics
3	Liability
4	Automobile Associations

Table 3: TCA Identified Themes - Legal and Regulatory Environment.

The first theme, legislations and regulations, covers six key categories: Leading countries, activities and development, legal sphere, ideal legal and regulatory environment, special permission, and taxonomy. At this point of the development, no clearly leading country can be identified as every system has its own advantages and disadvantages. Although, some experts see a slight advantage with respect to AD-level 3 and 4 in Germany and AD-level 5 in the USA. Analysing the legislative and regulatory activities reveal that heretofore Germany is the only one to adopt the Road Traffic Act to enable AD-level 3 and parts of AD-level 4. The USA also introduced various legislations, but it has to be distinguished between federal and state laws. On a federal level no specific Motor Vehicle Safety Standards (FMVSS) exist, as only a first set of principles as guidelines for AV development are issued. Due to the absence of federal laws and regulations, states issue their own laws and regulations such as California did which imposes challenges for companies to comply with. Apart from Germany and the USA, various other countries are actively considering and issuing laws and regulations for AVs such as Japan, the UK or China. The nationwide implementation of AD-level 4 in Germany can be time consuming as not only the national Road Traffic Act must be amended, but firstly the VC has to be changed. However, the VC is adopted approximately every 10 years which would not be sufficient for a nationwide implementation of AVs by 2025. An accelerator for a previous amend of the VC could be proven positive influences of AD technology on the number of accidents. Experts believe that AVs will be operating in Germany by 2025, but are most likely limited by their ODD (operational design domain). The experts' opinions diverge regarding having unified laws within the EU or the US. While some believe that various US state laws are not problematic but even create flexibility, others consider the different laws as extra work and challenging to monitor as well as to comply with. Therefore, unified laws are preferred that are initiated by one leading country and followed by others, also in the EU/ECE. But this is difficult to achieve due to the various interests of all stakeholders. In Germany as well as in the EU technological development follows legislations and regulations. A high-level of detail of technological descriptions are required for issuing laws and regulations but since the technology is not developed yet, this reduces and limits the speed of development. In the USA, laws and regulations are rather following technology and thus development is less regulated. But the quality associated with the output of the system is doubted by German experts. In fact, recent events in the USA support this concern as Uber stopped testing their ADCs in Arizona after a deadly accident in March 2018 (Bergen & Newcomer, 2018). Most German experts believe that laws and regulations limit the risk of OEMs to some extent and that for example deploying AVs in urban areas right away is more dangerous than starting out with less complex and comprehensive situations. Overall, it is not possible to clearly state if technology or the government should set the pace. Ideally would be a mixture of the German and the American system that sets guidelines and principles, is flexible while allows to make sound judgements and handle risk efficiently. Experts agree that it is vital to have an interactive matching process between technology as well as legislations and regulations towards the mutual optimum. Basically, testing AVs of any AD-level is not prohibited in Germany. Only a special permission needs to be issued by the authorities which is done by reviewing the presented testing concept as well as major guiding regulations such as the VC. The decision is made on a case by case basis and since the term 'driver' that is required by the VC can be differently interpreted, the outcome of the decision can vary by authority. The process of granting special permission is similar around the world, but might be more time consuming in Germany than in the USA. The process might be used in the future to enable the implementation of AVs in the beginning in Germany, in case an adoption of the VC in time fails. The taxonomy in form of the AD-levels are significant and vital for the differentiation of AD technology. The distinction between the AD-levels, especially AD-level 4 and 5 is vague and often people believe that AD-level 4 is including a conventional human driver while AD-level 5 is without one. In fact, AD-level 4 includes AD systems that operate with but can also operate without a conventional human driver in specific

ODDs while for AD-level 5 no conventional human driver is needed for any driving mode and consequently the AV is not limited by the ODD.

The second identified theme is ethics which includes ethical dilemmas and data security. Overall, experts consider ethical concerns as serious a topic but certain aspects such as ethical dilemmas are made more controversial by media. Implementing death preventing AD systems is considered to be ethical, though implementing it in every car and using it will not be mandatory in the early stage. Experts believe that ethical dilemmas will occur less with AVs as vehicles drive passively, breaks early and efficiently, and their systems are always active. Nevertheless, even the best prerequisites cannot prevent all accidents as some unforeseeable situations will occur. In general, AVs cannot solve the world's problem of ethical dilemmas. In these ethical dilemmas, AVs are not allowed to offset one life against another based on a person's feature including age, gender, and job. In a dangerous situation, the AV analyses the situation and may carry out an evasive manoeuvre in case no other collision will be caused. If a collision is unpreventable, the AV will simply break and reduce speed in order to limit the damage. The trolley problem, cannot and will not occur in the foreseeable future as the relevant information to classify people cannot be recorded. A further ethical concern is data security. Recording of data during a ride is regulated by the Road Traffic Act. For AD-level 3 various information is recorded on a memory system including records of who is driving (human or machine) as well as time and place of handing over the driving responsibility. Analyzing all recorded data with AI is not allowed, but would be necessary. On the one hand to learn and to ensure equal intelligence of every AV all the time. On the other hand in case of an accident in order to analyze and find the error to prevent further collision due to the same issue. Furthermore, recording and analyzing of any visual data is prohibited but is important in order to reconstruct accidents to increase transparency and legal certainty.

Liability is the third theme. This theme contains the categories liability system and collision. The German liability system consists of the vehicle owner, the vehicle driver and the vehicle manufacturer and is considered to be more sophisticated than in the USA as well as sufficient for the next AD-level (AD-level 3). For further AD-levels including AD-level 4 without a conventional human driver and AD-level 5, minor changes and adjustments might be necessary as only the vehicle owner and the OEM remain and no operator or driver can be held liable. In case of a collision, the liability system functions as follows. If an accident is caused due to an unavoidable situation the product insurance of the operator or driver covers the costs. For AD-level 3 and parts of AD-level 4, the driver remains responsible for the vehicle when actively driving while the vehicle owner is responsible for maintenance and may be held liable in case of an accident caused by neglecting his obligations. While, OEMs are liable for any accidents or damages caused by a technical failure of the AV. Though, the OEM may claim reimbursement from suppliers in case a supplier's part caused the collision. Experts believe that in case of a person's death, criminal prosecution will apply. The execution and judgement of criminal prosecutions are currently not foreseeable but are to be determined in the future.

The fourth theme is automobile associations including aim and purpose as well as responsibilities. For legal and regulatory concerns, automobile associations are also perceived as a platform for communication and discussion with politicians and international associations from different countries. Associations are a vital opportunity for German OEMs to connect, to share ideas (especially in the early stage of development) and to co-create regulatory decisions as associations are well connected to federal ministries and UN committees where suggestions for laws and regulations can be proposed. The platform further enables and gives the possibility for driving demonstrations including discussions with the government in order to educate politicians, imitate further thinking and to convince politicians by demonstrating the advantages of AD systems. Besides, associations take over certain responsibilities for its members such as negotiating in various matters including legislative and regulatory terms and standards. Furthermore, associations consult and guide legal and regulatory instances regarding legislative and technological considerations.

5.2 Quantitative Analysis

5.2.1 Customer readiness

The conducted survey on customer readiness contains 12 questions regarding AVs in addition to two personal statements (see Appendix F). The DV (depending variable) within the survey is the overall willingness to use AVs, which is influenced by various IVs (independent variables) that are investigated through the remaining questions. The original responses are partly coded in order to enable a numeric analysis. In total 64 people participated in the survey with an equal distribution between male and female. The vast majority (87,5%) of the respondents comes from urban areas and a small portion (12,5%) from rural regions. The participants' age range lies between 20 and 30 years and the histogram shows a peak at 23 years of age (see Appendix G)

Figure 6 illustrates the overall willingness of the respondents to use AVs. The answers are recorded on a range from 1 (not at all) to 5 (absolutely) and are almost normally distributed. The graph shows that only around 23% are averse to use of AVs, while the other 77% are willing or at least not averse of riding in an AV.

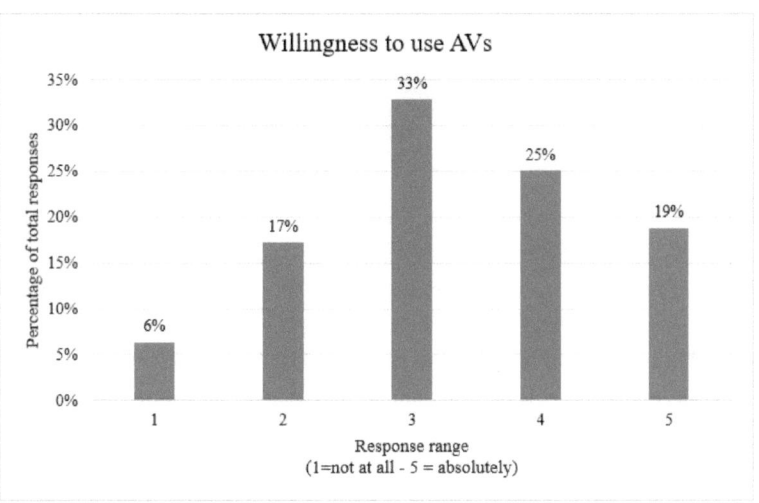

Figure 6. Willingness to use AVs.

Due to the difference in the means between male and female responses (delta = 0,53125), a t-test[6] with the pre-determined significant level of 5% is conducted. The output of the t-test shows that there is no statistically significant difference between the two groups, as P(T<=t) two tail is greater than 5% (0,0654) (see Appendix H).

The investigated willingness to give up one's own car and to only use AVs of mobility providers, is indicated by the following graph (Figure 7). Overall, the responses show that the majority (41%) are not willing to give up their car, even though full mobility coverage is assumed. Nevertheless, at least 23% are willing to give up their own car and another 36% are undecided.

---

[6] Hypotheses of the t-test: H_0: $\mu_{\text{male-female (willingness)}} = 0$ and H_1: $\mu_{\text{male-female (willingness)}} \neq 0$.

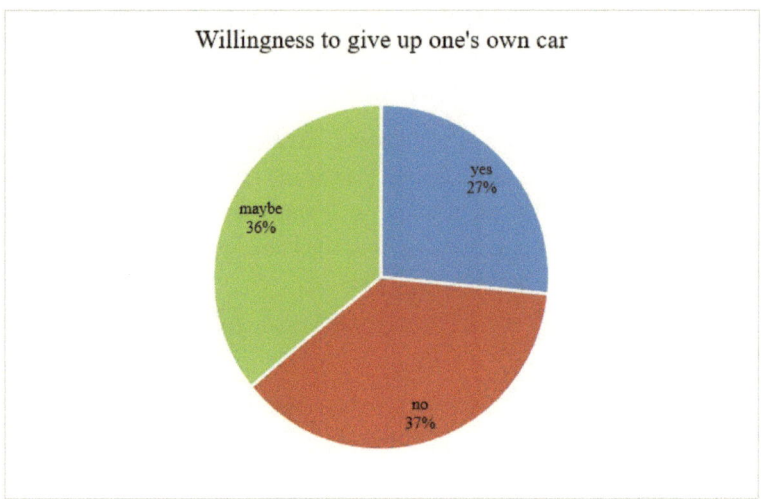

Figure 7. Willingness to give up one's own Car.

More precisely, the responses differ by gender as illustrated by Figure 8. Even though, slightly more male respondents (28% over 25%) are willing to replace their car, twice as many male participants reject to replace their own car with mobility solutions compared to female participants. Besides, females are much more open and willing to consider abandoning their personal vehicle than males (50% and 22% respectively).

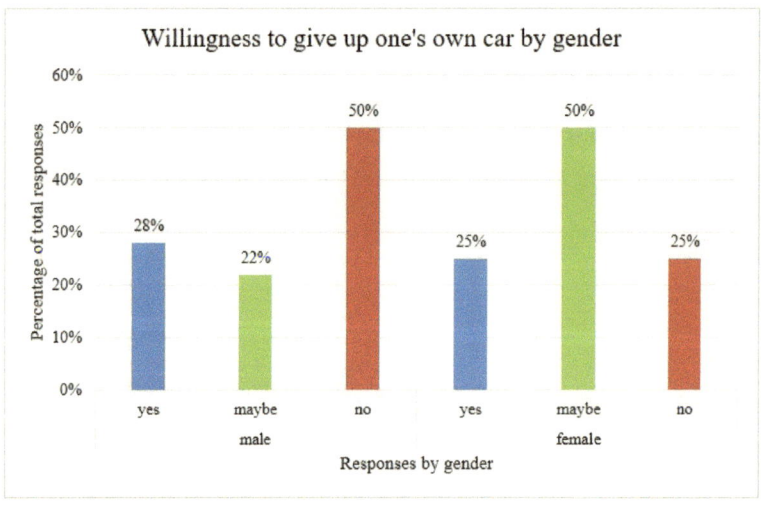

Figure 8. Willingness to give up one's own Car by Gender.

Primary Research Analysis

To validate the indication, a Chi-Square-test[7] with the significance level of 5% is conducted (see Table 4). Based on the extracted p-value (0,043998) which is below the selected significance level, H_0 can be rejected and consequently gender is related to and dependent on the willingness to give up one's own car.

Chi-Square				
	yes	maybe	no	total
male	0,02941176	1,76086957	1,33333333	3,12361466
female	0,02941176	1,76086957	1,33333333	3,12361466
total	0,05882353	3,52173913	2,66666667	6,24722933
df	2			
p-val	0,04399784			

Table 4: Chi-Square-Test of Gender and Willingness to give up one's own Car.

To further investigate the findings, an ANOVA[8] with a significance level of 5 % is conducted for male and female participants on the willingness to give up one's own car. While the analysis for females shows no difference on the willingness to give up the car based on the driving experience and fun (p-value about 0,8307 (see Appendix I)), it is the opposite for male candidates (see Table 5). As the p-value (smaller 5%) indicates, H_0 can be rejected and males' willingness to give up one's own car is significantly influenced by the driving experience and fun.

ANOVA						
Source of Variation	SS	df	MS	F	P-value	F crit
Between Groups	11,36161	2	5,680803571	4,133345	0,02634021	3,327654499
Within Groups	39,85714	29	1,374384236			
Total	51,21875	31				

Table 5: Anova on Willingness to give up one's own Car and Importance of Driving Experience for Male Participants.

---

[7] Hypotheses of the Chi-Square-test: H_0: Gender and willingness to give up one's own car are independent (unrelated) and H_1: Gender and willingness to give up one's own car are related.

[8] Hypotheses for Anova: H_0: $\mu_{willing\ to\ give\ up\ the\ car\ -\ yes} = \mu_{willing\ to\ give\ up\ the\ car\ -maybe} = \mu_{willing\ to\ give\ up\ the\ car\ -\ no}$ and H_1: $\mu_{willing\ to\ give\ up\ the\ car\ -\ yes} \neq \mu_{willing\ to\ give\ up\ the\ car\ -\ maybe} \neq \mu_{willing\ to\ give\ up\ the\ car\ -\ no}$.

The following Figure 9 shows a ranking of ten daily mobility factors. The factors are evaluated on a scale from 1 (not important at all) to 5 (of utmost importance). The social status is considered to be the least important factor by far, while safety is perceived as most vital.

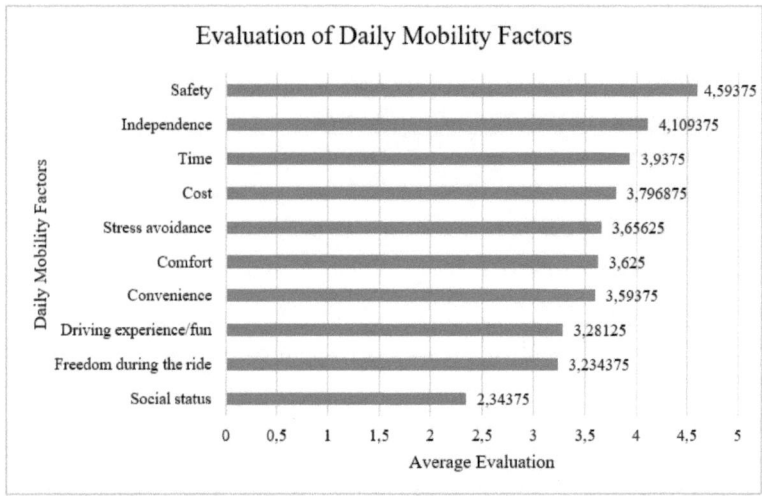

Figure 9. Evaluation of Daily Mobility Factors.

Overall, about half of the respondents (52%) indicated no concerns regarding riding in a vehicle without manual steering possibilities. Though, the consequent assumption that this portion prefers specially designed AVs or has no preferences, is proven false. The Figure 10 shows that the preference for conventional vehicles with AD-ability applies for both groups. In total, only 13% prefer specially designed AVs.

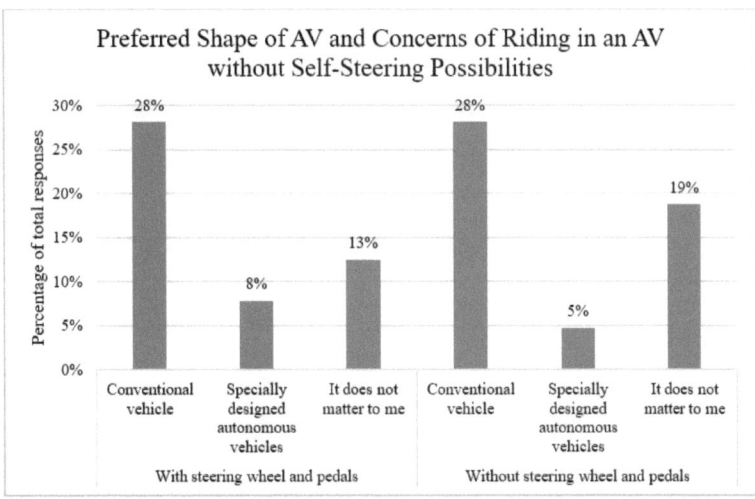

Figure 10. Preferred Shape of AV and Concerns of Riding in an AV without Self-Steering Possibilities.

Aggregated, the responses for the safety considerations of AVs indicate an equal level of safety for passengers and pedestrians (mean about 3,05 and 3 respectively). Thus, AVs are perceived to be on average, on the same safety level as current vehicles. This is illustrated by Figure 11. The chart also shows that slightly more respondents consider AVs to be safer than current vehicles (indicated by the responses with 4).

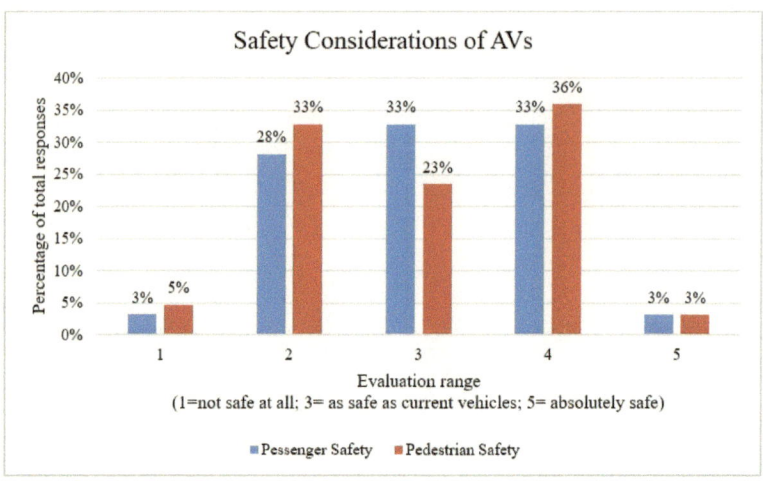

Figure 11. Safety Considerations of AVs.

Close to two-third of the respondents considered traditional OEMs to be more trustworthy than newcomers (new AV providers) regarding the conception of AVs (see Figure 12). Nevertheless, one-third believes both are on the same level and neither traditional OEMs nor newcomers have an advantage.

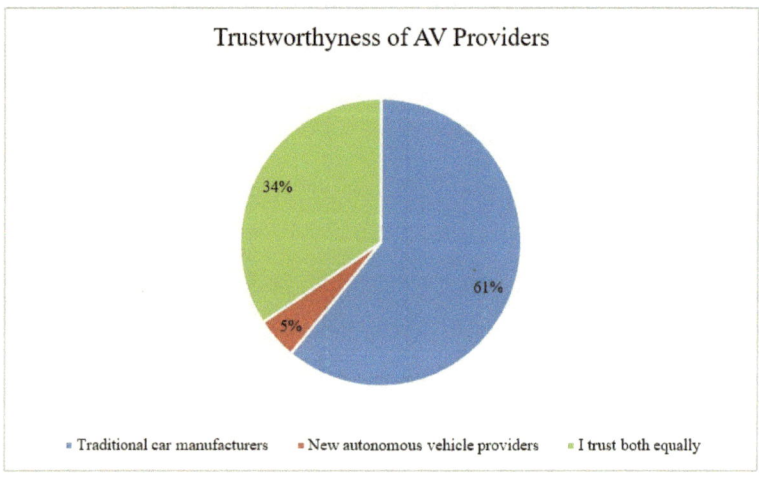

Figure 12. Trustworthiness of AV Providers.

Figure 13 below, displays the fear of the respondents concerning cyberattacks on AVs. While around two-third (63%) are in fear, a fair proportion of 14% is unsure of the potential danger. Nevertheless, 23% do not fear cyberattacks on AVs.

Fear of Cyberattack on AVs

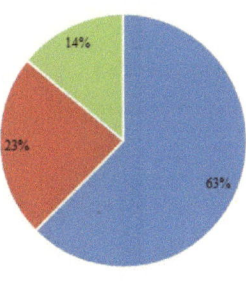

Figure 13. Fear of Cyberattacks on AVs.

The influence of positive and negative news on the opinion of the male respondents regarding AVs is indicated by the following Figure 14. With an average evaluation of about 2,78, male respondents are rather weakly influenced by media in both positive and negative ways. Though in terms of frequency, the majority (38%) is strongly influenced by negative media.

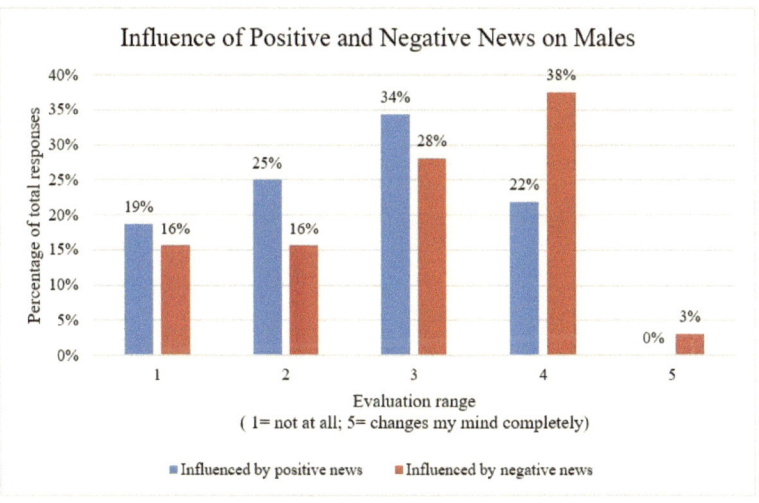

Figure 14. Influence of Positive and Negative News on Males.

In contrary to male respondents, females are more influenced by media (average evaluation of around 3,54) as Figure 15 illustrates in form of a left-skewed shape. The graph indicates a greater influence of negative news over positive news on

53

females. Nevertheless, the peak in terms of frequency is on positive news as 47% of the female respondents are strongly influenced.

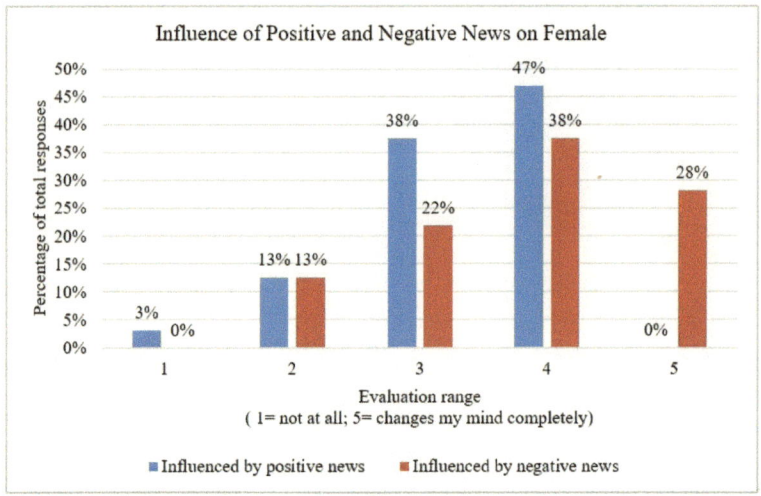

Figure 15. Influence of Positive and Negative News on Females.

The difference of the detected delta in the means between males and females is further investigated with a t-test[9] (significance level 5%). The results are statistically significant as P(T<=t) two tail is about 4,657E-05. Consequently, H_0 can be rejected and therefore males and females are differently affected and influenced by news on AVs (see Table 6).

---

[9] Hypotheses of the t-test: H_0: $\mu_{male\text{-}female\ (influence\ of\ positive\ and\ negative\ news)}$ = 0 and H_1: $\mu_{male\text{-}female\ (influence\ of\ positive\ and\ negative\ news)}$ ≠ 0.

t-Test: Two-Sample Assuming Equal Variances		
	Male	Female
Mean	2,78125	3,546875
Variance	1,221230159	0,886657
Observations	64	64
Pooled Variance	1,053943452	
Hypothesized Mean Difference	0	
df	126	
t Stat	-4,218736886	
P(T<=t) one-tail	2,32876E-05	
t Critical one-tail	1,657036982	
P(T<=t) two-tail	4,65752E-05	
t Critical two-tail	1,978970602	

Table 6: T-test on Influence of Positive and Negative News of AVs on Gender.

Further t-test[10] regarding the influence of positive and negative news on both males and females is conducted individually with a significance level of 5%. The output shows statistically significant results for females only, as males are not significantly influenced (see Appendix J). With a value of P(T<=t) two tail smaller than 5% (around 0,0228) H₀ can be rejected and the superior influence of negative over positive news on female respondents is proven to be significant (see Table 7).

---

[10] Hypotheses of the t-test: H_0: $\mu_{positive,\ negative\ news\ (female)} = 0$ and H_1: $\mu_{positive,\ negative\ news\ (female)} \neq 0$.

t-Test: Two-Sample Assuming Equal Variances		
	How much would you be influenced in your opinion on autonomous vehicles by positive newspaper articles (e.g. no accident in the last year)?	How much would you be influenced in your opinion on autonomous vehicles by negative newspaper articles (e.g. another horror crash in an autonomous vehicle, several people dead)?
Mean	3,28125	3,8125
Variance	0,660282258	0,995967742
Observations	32	32
Pooled Variance	0,828125	
Hypothesized Mean Difference	0	
df	62	
t Stat	-2,335129587	
P(T<=t) one-tail	0,011394235	
t Critical one-tail	1,669804163	
P(T<=t) two-tail	0,022788469	
t Critical two-tail	1,998971517	

Table 7: T-test on the Influence of Positive and Negative News of AVs on Females.

The believed knowledge level of males and females about AVs is illustrated by the following Figure 16. The pillars for male respondents indicate a nearly normal distribution, with a peak of 38% at an average knowledge (responded with 3). On the contrary, the curve of the female responses is right skewed which indicates an overall lower knowledge level and the peak of female responses, is at a low knowledge level (responded with 2) which account for 53% of the participants.

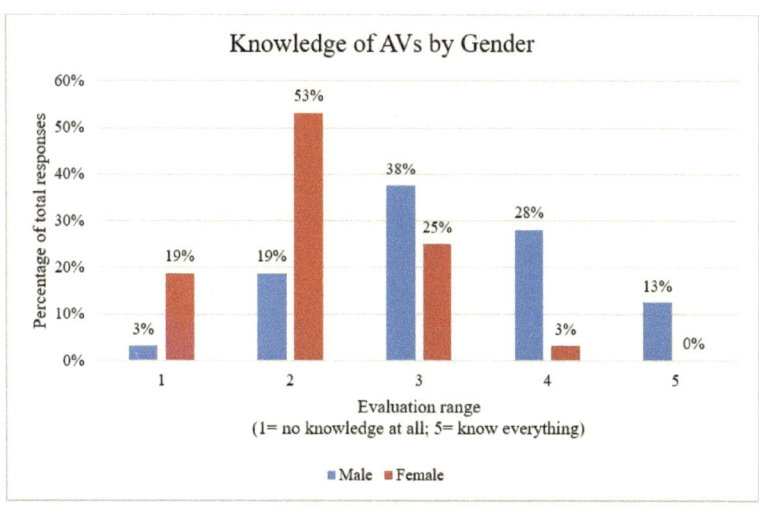

Figure 16. Knowledge of AVs by Gender.

The difference in the means between male and female respondents is significant as the following output of the t-test[11] shows (see Table 8). Since the P(T<=t) two tail value is around 2,842E-06, H_0 can be rejected and males consider themselves to be more educated about AVs than females.

---

[11] Hypotheses of the t-test: H_0: $\mu_{male, female\ (knowledge\ of\ AVs)} = 0$ and H_1: $\mu_{male, female\ (knowledge\ of\ AVs)} \neq 0$.

t-Test: Two-Sample Assuming Equal Variances		
	Male	Female
Mean	3,28125	2,125
Variance	1,04737903	0,56451613
Observations	32	32
Pooled Variance	0,80594758	
Hypothesized Mean Difference	0	
df	62	
t Stat	5,15179222	
P(T<=t) one-tail	1,421E-06	
t Critical one-tail	1,66980416	
P(T<=t) two-tail	2,842E-06	
t Critical two-tail	1,99897152	

Table 8: Difference in Knowledge of AVs by Gender.

6 Discussion

6.1 Technology

The TCA analysis revealed several themes which are overlapping and interdependent. Overall, the competition of developing AVs is open and ongoing on a national as well as an international level. In general, no clear leading country or company can be identified at this stage of the development process. Consequently, German OEMs neither have a significant advantage nor disadvantage at the moment. However, single companies have specific competitive edges such as Waymo in testing AVs, Daimler and Bosch with their R&D knowledge and budget, and Audi with its advanced sensor system.

New competitors are entering the industry of AV mobility, reshaping the value chain and introducing innovative business models. Newcomers are usually not aiming to build entire AVs, but to rather specialize in the AD system and market operation. Their aim is to become the new link to the end-users and as a consequence push current OEMs down in the value chain and make them first-tier suppliers. In general, it is perceived that a position right at the customer is very beneficial as it offers a high real net output ratio and significant market power can be gained. Therefore, German OEMs have to reconsider and change their strategy and market position. As a consequence, most are aiming to become mobility providers by building and operating AVs. But, it is essential to consider that this results in a target conflict among the subsidiaries or divisions within OEMs. While the subsidiary or division responsible for AV manufacturing aims to sell as many AVs as possible, the subsidiary or division which operates the AVs aims to deploy as few AVs as possible while offering their customers a certain level of mobility. Yet, to successfully achieve this transformation it is highly recommended to continue to pursue a dual strategy of developing both conventional vehicles with AD-ability and specially designed AVs. Although in the premium and luxury sport segment, specially designed AVs may be less relevant as the value of sport drive would be lost. In this specific sport segment, offering a hybrid of sport drive experience and AD-comfort is vital. It is important to mention that conventional vehicles with AD-ability and specially designed AVs will differ in the beginning with respect to the AD-ability. Conventional vehicles with AD-ability will have a less sophisticated AD system compared to specially designed AVs. Sharing models will increase the efficiency drastically, but sharing models have to be differentiated. Conventional vehicles with AD-ability may be shared among end-users and originally belong to individual people or car sharing companies. Whereas specially designed AVs will likely be owned by specific operators or subsidiaries of OEMs due to the high costs and only be shared by end-users as common small buses or taxis today.

A reshape of the industry's value chain requires German OEMs to adopt the strategy and to build new competitive advantages as current core capabilities such as building ICEs are becoming obsolete. New competitive advantages need to be built not only in AD but also in the remaining megatrends of connected, shared and electric in order to gain synergies and developed effective AVs. Developing new competitive advantages require resources and in order to ensure an efficient investment, German OEMs should focus on specific research areas. The research areas need to correlate with the overall strategy and position of the company. Certain R&D areas are less relevant while others are already sufficiently covered by top-tier German suppliers such as Continental or Bosch. Thus, German OEMs should focus on and aim to build competitive advantages in the area of sensor systems including AI. But, it is important to differentiate between the single components. Top-tier suppliers are specialized in building sophisticated sensors, though limitations exist. For example, generally a deployment of AVs, 365 days a year in 2025 is considered to be rather unrealistic. Therefore, German OEMs need to add value by integrating each sensor system and developing AI that analyses and interprets the input of all connected sensors and operates the vehicle holistically. Even though communication to infrastructure can be seen as part of the sensor system (external input), it is considered to be not vital and can be neglected, especially in the beginning when considering that building smart infrastructure including highways and traffic lights is expensive and time consuming. On the contrary, cybersecurity is a relevant factor that requires attention, but it is considered to be more of a requirement that has to be fulfilled than a possible factor for establishing a competitive advantage. All in all German OEMs should continue to utilize the power of associations in order to set standards, collaborate and create synergies with suppliers and other stakeholders such as the government or end-users. With regards to AVs, OEMs have to consider various specifications. Since the requirements differ by deployment and ownership, OEMs should build use case specific AVs. Because the targeted end-users' needs differ in intercity sections compared to urban areas and personally owned AVs should offer different advantages than specially designed AVs. In accordance with the dual strategy, personally owned AVs should be conventional vehicles with AD-ability in order to enable and offer autonomous as well as manual steering options in the beginning. While in specially designed AVs, no manual steering options should be equipped because it is not adding value due to the use case. Overall, OEMs need to focus on offering mobility packages, this applies for personally owned and specially designed AVs. For specially designed AVs which should start out in urban areas, the integration in the mobility environment, for example integrating the application in an aggregator or meta platform is necessary. Otherwise, abandoning the own vehicle and switching to mobility providers is less attractive for end-users. Furthermore, OEMs need to be aware that AVs have to have different attributes and fulfil other needs. The integration of the living and working environment in the vehicle becomes more important as the driving task is partially or fully taken over by the vehicle. Thus, enabling a customer specific utilization of the travelling time will be a critical factor and OEMs should partner up with firms such as Microsoft or Sony and build well-functioning interfaces. Specially designed AVs have to offer an increase in efficiency regarding time as well as costs and the usability needs to be convenient for end-users in terms of availability and close pick up locations. Every AV needs to be safe and secure. With respect to safety, Waymo is deemed to have an advantage over German OEMs as the company has more testing kilometres and accident-free testing can be associated with quality and safety of the system. Consequently, German OEMs should increase their testing efforts and make them transparent in order to prove their AVs' quality and reliability. Further, it is necessary that German OEMs exploit the current advantages and transfer their brand values to AD in order to differentiate themselves, reduce end-users' sceptic and enable a brand based identification with AVs.

6.2 Legal and Regulatory Environment

The conducted TCA analysis revealed four themes that are interdependent, influence each other and cannot be considered separately. Overall, the taxonomy and definition of the AD-levels helped in order to create a common understanding of the different AD-abilities of a vehicle, on a national as well as an international level. Although the differentiation between the AD-levels 4 and 5 is indistinct and often people believe that AD-level 4 includes a conventional driver while AD-level 5 does not. In fact, AD-level 4 includes AD-systems that operate with but can also operate without a conventional human driver in limited ODDs. While AD-level 5 is considered as a final stage of development or target of the AD-abilities as no conventional human driver is needed anymore for any driving mode. Consequently, the AV is not limited by the ODD. As along as an AV is not able to cover all driving modes, it cannot achieve AD-level 5. But this does not imply that an AV of AD-level 4 cannot perform all necessary driving modes without a conventional human driver within an ODD such as a defined urban area. As a consequence, AD-level 5 will not be realized within the decade as all constructed AVs are likely to be limited by some driving modes or the ODD including speed and driving environment in the beginning. The difficulty of differentiating AD-level 4 and 5 is likely going to diminish and become clearer over time as different AVs are being introduced. Nevertheless, a distinct differentiation between the various AVs based on the AD-level is going to be difficult since the AD-level 4 covers a wide range of AD-abilities. As a matter of fact AVs in which the systems covers the fallback performance of dynamic tasks are deemed to be AD-level 4 but may vary dramatically by their ODD. For example, could one AV only be able to drive autonomously on a specific small area within Stuttgart while another AV is able to drive autonomously in the entire Stuttgart area, both are considered as AVs with AD-level 4 ability because both have a limited ODD. Consequently, a more sophisticated differentiation regarding the ODDs of AVs is required.

All in all, no leading or superior legal and regulatory environment for the development of AVs can be identified at the current stage of development. Every system is associated with specific advantages and disadvantages, similar to the consideration of unified versus individual laws and regulations within a country or an economic union. While unified laws and regulations enable a wider application, less monitoring work for OEMs, and more legal certainty, it also reduces the speed of development as individual laws allow a faster implementation and testing. Certain is, that neither the EU nor the USA has the ideal legal and regulatory environment. Perceived as ideal is a hybrid of both systems that sets guidelines and principles, is flexible while allows to make sound judgements and handle risk efficiently. But more important than the system is to have an iterative matching process of both the technological development as well as the legal and regulatory environment in order to build an intact system at a mutual optimum. Though no ideal legal and regulatory environment exists, Germany can be seen as a pioneer in the EU as it is currently the only country with an amended Road Traffic Act. In the future development, it is important for Germany, on the one hand to proceed with the national development in order to stay ahead of other competing countries such as China or the USA and on the other hand to become a role model and further initiate the development in the entire EU. In order to adopt the German

Road Traffic Act, firstly the VC must be changed, but this can be time consuming. Therefore, adoptions need to be made within the next few years in order to enable further changes in the German Road Traffic Act and eventually a nationwide implementation of AVs by 2025. Changing the VC depends on the agreement of various parties and in order to convince them, automobile associations can be utilized. Automobile associations as a platform should continuously be used to discuss, collaborate and share ideas and visions among politicians, OEMs, suppliers, and other stakeholders. Discussions and possibilities for driving demonstration should be utilized to convince participants of the positive impact and influence of AD on the reduction of accidents and road deaths. Further discussions are needed concerning the term 'driver' which is a key term that is used in the VC as well as many other regulations. While the meaning of this term was simple in the past, it becomes inherently difficult to define in the future. The reason is, that for parts of AD-level 4 no conventional human driver will exist as the system carries out the driving responsibility. The driver is a central part of the VC and the national Road Traffic Acts, but it has to be clarified and defined what a 'driver' is and if a driver can only be a human or also a machine in the future. Further on, the ideas, discussion, and conclusion should be shared on an international level with foreign automobile associations in order to initiate similar discussions in further EU countries. In case an adoption of the VC cannot be made before the planned introduction of the first AVs, a solution for OEMs could be to apply for special permission as testing any AD-level in Germany is generally not prohibited and decisions are made case by case. Since in the beginning AVs are limited by their ODD, a special permission could be sufficient for OEMs in order to be able to proceed with development and to be granted first deployments of the technology.

The liability system is considered to be sufficient for the next AD-level and only minor changes might be necessary for AD-level 4 without a conventional human driver. Therefore, OEMs do not need to intensively promote and advance the liability consideration, but with respect to ethics, it is necessary. It is clear that AVs cannot solve the world's problem of ethical dilemmas as on the one hand choosing between the lives of people based on personal features is prohibited and on the other hand collecting the relevant personal information through sensors is not possible today and will not be possible in the foreseeable future. It is set that in a dangerous situation AVs primarily breaks but can carry out evasive manoeuvres in case no collision is caused. But the handling and procedure of all recorded data is not sufficient. While various information is recorded, OEMs are missing permission for recording visual data for restructuring accidents and creating legal certainty as well as accessing and analysing all recorded data to improve the overall intelligence of their AVs. In order to improve the development and AVs' AI, accessing and analysing all data is fundamental. As big data is incredibly important, German OEMs should initiate further considerations and discussion with the government on data security and data accessing rights for OEMs.

6.3 Customer Readiness

The analysis of the customer readiness shows that most millennials are neither affectionate nor averse to use AVs, irrespectively of gender. Nevertheless, a minority of the people is extremely willing or not at all willing to use AVs. The willingness to use AVs does not differ by gender, the likeliness to give up one's own car and to only use autonomous mobility solutions from mobility service providers highly varies between men and women. Since women are less refusing and more open to giving up their car, females are the primary target of mobility providers. However, the majority of women are yet undecided, similar to the overall willingness of all people to use AVs. As most people do not have a sophisticated opinion today, OEMs have the chance to positively influence their opinion and decision. Influencing the population and increasing the technology acceptance as well as the adoption of AVs can be executed simultaneously in two ways. Firstly, by designing AVs according to end-users' preferences and needs. Secondly, by educating and letting people experience AVs and their advantages.

Firstly, the greater the product, the higher the acceptance. Thus, it is vital to constantly improve and design the service of mobility that is distributed through AVs, in accordance with the needs of end-users. The inclusion or abolition of a steering wheel and pedals is currently a fifty-fifty decision. But the acceptance of having no manual steering options is likely to increase with time as well as a widely adoption and experience of AD-levels. At the current stage of development the majority prefers to drive conventional vehicles with AD-ability compared to riding in specially designed AVs. Therefore, German OEMs should continue to equip their latest models with AD-level 3 and afterward AD-level 4 technology. This enables owners and users, to experience the advantages of automated driving when desired, while not losing the driving experience and fun which is especially important for males. Continuing with a hybrid strategy is also vital from a customer's point of view as still one-third do not have a preference regarding a conventional or specially designed AV. OEMs should also offer mobility services by oper-

Discussion

ating specially designed AVs in specific urban areas. The analysis of people's key daily mobility factors reveals significant differences in the importance and value of various factors. Consequently, AVs have to be constructed and cover certain mobility requirements differently than conventional vehicles. While some key attributes need to be bold, others can be neglected. This enables significant changes not only in the construction and design of AVs, but also with respect to the ecosystem of a holistic mobility service. The most valued attributes that an AV should offer are safety, independence and time efficiency. Currently most people are afraid of possible cyberattacks and perceive AVs to be only as safe as conventional vehicles. Thus, increasing and improving the overall safety of AVs for passengers and pedestrians compared to conventional vehicles, can increase the acceptance and usage of AVs. Moreover, safety and quality of driving could be future key competitive advantages and differentiation factors for German OEMs. Independence is a further vital factor in people's mobility requirements that an AV has to cover. A car gives the owner or the driver the ability to go anywhere at any time. It is necessary, that AVs are maintaining this high-level of independence, irrespectively of whether the AVs is personally owned or used via a mobility service provider. As time is the third most valued factor, pickup locations for shared AVs need to be close and AVs in general have to be efficient in going from place A to place B. Intelligent routing systems which analyse current and anticipate future traffic congestion are necessary in order to reduce the duration of the journey. Though, cost, stress avoidance, comfort, and convenience are not the most critical factors, considering these is indispensable. The costs of a product always influence an ordinary buyer's decision as almost all people are price sensitive at some point. That means the TCO of an AV or the TCU (total cost of usage) of a robotaxi of a mobility service providers, must be in an acceptable price range compared to the TCO of a conventional vehicle or the TCU of current taxi services. Furthermore, stress avoidance, comfort and convenience have to be in accordance with the primary target group as these factors may differ from the general population of 20 to 30 year olds. For example, for a business person stress avoidance, comfort and convenience are much more important than the costs compared to an ordinary person. Despite the overall low importance of the driving experience and the freedom during the ride, especially men's willingness to give up their own car is significantly influenced by the driving experience. While this has a negative impact on the usage of robotaxis, it highly favours conventional vehicles with AD-ability. OEMs were able to exploit the power of the social status in order to sale premium vehicles, however exploiting this power is expected to diminish over time as it has little relevance for millennials.

Secondly, the greater the education and the experience of AVs, the greater the technology acceptance and the customer readiness. While in the beginning a disruptive technology may be perceived as controversially, educating and letting people experience the new technology can turnaround the image. In total, the population is not well educated about AVs and females believe to know less than males. Due to that, increasing the overall knowledge of AVs including the related advantages of the technology is necessary in order to fully capitalize on the gained advantages of this disruptive technology. For example, one major advantage of the new technology is that AVs are safer and causing fewer accidents as the mistakes caused by humans are eliminated. However, end-users are currently either not aware or not convinced by this as they perceive AVs to be only as safe as manual vehicles for passengers and pedestrians. Therefore, education is vital. More impressively and convincing than audio or visual education, is the first-hand experience of the technology. Demonstrating the advantages in public and having people experience the technology for free, is the key to convince people. In general, the education of AVs should be carried out with specific focus on females in order to offset the difference and to capitalize on females' openness to replace their car by autonomous mobility service solutions. Another important factor to consider, especially during the development and early life cycle phase of AVs is the influence of media. People are forming their opinions by hearing and reading news. Men are less affected by news regarding AVs than women and women are more influenced by negative than positive news. This is important for German OEMs to keep in mind when making the risk assessment for further commercializing actions, as the influence of news articles can either be supportive or impending on the customer readiness. A great advantage that German OEMs have compared to Waymo and other newcomers, is that the majority of the Germans consider them to be more trustworthy. Consequently, this can be a further key asset as the associated attributes of safety, trust, and quality are valued the most.

6.4 Key Recommendation for German OEMs

The investigated research areas are critical pillars for the overall success of the technology. The pillars are necessary and influence each other and only if success is reached in the technological development, a functioning legal and regulatory system is established and customers are offered attractive mobility solutions, the emerging technology can be implemented. Figure 17 illustrates the summarized key recommendations in each pillar for enabling a successful transformation to the future of AVs:

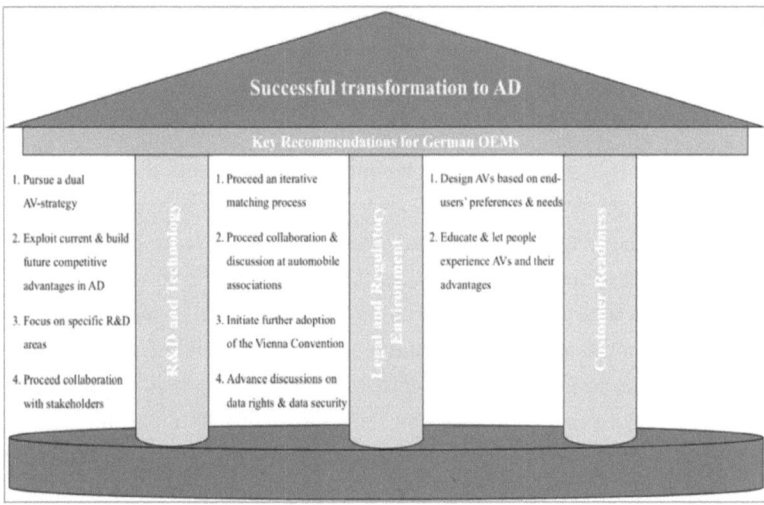

Figure 17. Key Recommendation for German OEMs.

The research paper revealed the development status, showed that the transformation process is ongoing while many challenges remain and German OEMs have to overcome various barriers in order to successfully implement AVs and secure the future of the German automobile industry.

7 Guidance for Future Research

7.1 Theoretical and Methodological Limitations

The research project underlies certain theoretical limitations. Due to the timewise limitation and complexity of the research domain, the scope of the paper is limited. Covering the entire topic is not possible and therefore only the most critical areas are investigated.

The research is designed to minimize methodological limitations as described in the methodology section. However, every methodology is limited to some extent and thus further adoptions could have been made in order to improve the validity and reliability of the research project: Qualitative research was conducted with OEMs and an automobile association, a further source of information from the government could add further valuable insights and validate the findings. Objectively, bias has to be considered with respect to the gained knowledge and insights from the conducted interviews since the interview partners are working for German OEMs or an automobile association. As a result, the interview partners might believe more in the success of the technology, hence are more positive and enthusiastic in their expressions regarding the importance, utilization, and chances of realization of the technology. Since various interviews were conducted via telephone or Skype, the gained insights are limited to verbal expressions as no assessment of body language or facial expression was possible. Due to the scope of the research project, only a few interviews could be conducted which limits the ability to generalize the gained insights. With respect to the customer survey, the conclusions are limited and can only be referred to the targeted survey population and thus cannot be generalized for all Germans. Besides, the number of randomly selected people from rural areas is insufficient for a thorough comparison between people from urban and rural areas. End-users' opinions may also differ by their geographic living place within German (different cities and states). As no specific data has been collected related to this aspect, possible differences could not be identified.

7.2 Suggestions for Future Research

The paper uncovered the current stage of development in the investigated research areas. Nevertheless, future research is required for mainly three reasons. Firstly, due to the purpose of the project, the research areas are covered in breadth but not in-depth and yet many details are to be revealed within each specific area. Secondly, the development of AVs is continuing and constantly new insights are discovered which need to be academically analysed and put into context. Thirdly, this paper revealed various challenges and barriers which should be further investigated and researched. Based on the findings in this paper, future research should focus on the following areas:

Firstly, regarding technology. In order to generalize the findings and insights from interviews, quantitative research should be conducted with OEMs, automobile associations, and other stakeholders. All findings and insights which are identified in the corresponding categories and themes can be further researched upon and detailed in various ways. For example, the analysis revealed that OEMs consider certain R&D areas to be highly relevant for AD and thus specifically analysing the supply chain including points of R&D differentiation of OEMs and suppliers can be valuable in order to identify key profitable research areas. As the sensor system including AI is deemed to be the most critical R&D area, detailed investigations regarding the specific technological limitations and advantages of German OEMs and suppliers compared to foreign firms should be made. As the development and competition proceeds, the countries, companies, and competition should be continuously monitored and analysed. The change and development of the value chain including the position, business models, and revenue streams of the players should also be further analysed as today sustainable business models are yet to be defined.

Secondly, the legal and regulatory environment. In general, the development of the legal and regulatory environment should be constantly monitored, not only in Germany but also in other competing countries. Adoptions of the VC were made in the past and further changes are required. In future research projects, the mechanism and procedure as well as the current status of changing the VC should be investigated in order to analyse the development, influencing factors, and the relevant setting lever. Data security and data accessing rights are critical for German OEMs. Therefore, detailed research in the legal situation and current discussions within future research papers is important. While the general doubts regarding the validity of the German liability system are eliminated, the execution and potential judgements for criminal prosecution (in case an AV causes death of a human) have to be defined.

Thirdly, customer readiness. The research discovered various factors which influence customers' readiness to use AVs. Further factors might play an important role for the customer readiness. With respect to the targeted respondents, a different age group could be analysed in order to gain a better understanding of the influence of age on the customer readiness. Nevertheless, the same analysis should be made with the same target group over a certain period of time in order to analyse and understand the development and progress. Besides, as immobile people including handicapped and older people are supposed to regain mobility through AD, their needs and demand for AVs need be researched and eventually be considered by German OEMs. Further investigations could be made regarding the influence of media, as well as the design of specially designed AVs.

As the development proceeds and companies are making progress, the research should be repeated after some time in order to monitor the general development and to address adjustments in critical lagging areas. The paper references to the development on an international level at certain points, but the main focus lies on Germany with respect to the raised primary data. To enable an adequate comparison on an international level, further research should be conducted in other countries such as the USA, China, and the UK as well as for competing companies such as Waymo or GM.

7.3 Personal Reflection of the Paper

This research project on AVs in Germany gives an overview of the status quo on an aggregated level and enabled me to make great gains in understanding the situation and current challenges of AD. In order to achieve the outcome various barriers had to be overcome and reflecting on the progress, certain improvements could have been made. The project schedule was accurate and many milestones were reached in time. However, the estimation of the duration of the primary research was not accurate as conducting all interviews and handling the transcript progress was more time consuming than expected. Planned interview partners were unavailable at that time or left the company and finding new respondents and a suitable timeframe was difficult. A further difficulty lay within the definition and understanding behind the AD-levels, specifically the differentiation between AD-level 4 and 5. Even the experts' understanding varied and caused some confusion in the beginning of the interviews. Therefore, it is advisable and it would have been better to synchronize the common understanding of the AD-levels in the beginning of each interview. Reflecting upon the conducted research project, I am satisfied with respect to the covered scope and outcome of the paper. I am confident that the research and the gained achievements are valuable contributions to the long and vital process of realizing and commercializing AVs in Germany.

References

Abbott, M. L., & McKinney, J. (2013). Understanding and Applying Research Design. New Jersey: Wiley.

Abdu-Dalbouh, H. M. (2013). A Questionnaire Approach based on the Technology Acceptance Model for Mobile Tracking on Patient Progress Applications. Journal of Computer Science, 9(6), 763-770.

Abraham, H., Lee, C., Brady, S., Fitzgerald, C., Mehler, B., Reimer, B., & Coughlin, J. F. (2016). Autonomous Vehicles, Trust, and Driving Alternatives: A Survey of Consumer Preferences. MIT AgeLab, 6, 1-16.

Abuelsamid, S. (2017). The Future For Smaller Automakers May Be As Tier 1 Suppliers To Apple And Waymo. Retrieved August 26, 2017, from Forbes: https://www.forbes.com/sites/samabuelsamid/2017/06/13/the-future-for-smaller-automakers-may-be-as-tier-1-suppliers-to-apple-and-waymo/#74148ee3f2fa

Alexander, D. (2013). How Self-Driving Cars Will Change The World. Retrieved July 29, 2017, from Forbes: https://www.forbes.com/sites/pikeresearch/2013/11/13/how-self-driving-cars-will-change-the-world/#55dd06266384

Anderson, J. M., Kalra, N., Stanley, K. D., Sorensen, P., Samaras, C., & Oluwatola, O. A. (2016). Autonomous Vehicle Technology. A Guide for Policymakers. Santa Monica: RAND.

Ang, S. H. (2014). Research Design. Los Angeles: SAGE.

AnnualReports.com. (2017). Annual Reports. Retrieved October 15, 2017, from General Motors: http://www.annualreports.com/Company/general-motors

Arthur D. Little. (2009). Future of Mobility 2020: Whither the Automotive Industry? online. Retrieved from Arthur D. Little: http://www.adlittle.com/downloads/tx_adlreports/ADL_Future_of_Mobility_2020.pdf

Attias, D. (2017). The Automobile Revolution. Towards a New Electro-Mobility Paradigm. New York: Springer.

Awad, E. M., & Ghaziri, H. M. (2007). Knowledge Management. New Delhi: Pearson.

References

Balnaves, M., & Caputi, P. (2001). Introduction to Quantitative Research Methods: An Investigative Approach. London: SAGE.

Banham, R. (2002). The Ford Century: Ford Motor Company and the Innovations that Shaped the World. New York: Artisan.

Bargende, M., Reuss, H.-C., & Wiedemann, J. (2017). 17. International Stuttgarter Symposium: Automobil- und Motorentechnik [17th Stuttgart International Symposium: Automotive and Engine Technolgy]. 17th Stuttgart International Symposium: Automotive and Engine Technolgy (pp. 1-176). Heidelberg: Springer.

BBC. (2015, October 08). Who is responsible for a driverless car accident? Retrieved November 01, 2017, from BBC News: http://www.bbc.com/news/technology-34475031.

Beidel, D. C., Frueh, C., & Hersen, M. (2014). Adult Psychopathology and Diagnosis. London: Wiley.

Beiker, S. (2013). The Cars we'll be Driving in the world of 2050. Retrieved December 29, 2017, from BBC: http://www.bbc.com/future/story/20131108-what-will-we-be-driving-in-2050.

Berger, M., & Newcomer, E. (2018) Uber Halts Autonomous Car Tests After Fatal Crash in Arizona. Retrieved March 20, 2018, from Bloomberg: https://www.bloomberg.com/news/articles/2018-03-19/uber-autonomous-car-involved-in-fatal-crash-in-arizona.

Blumberg, B. F., Cooper, D. R., & Schindler, P. S. (2014). Business Research Methods (4th edition ed.). London: McGraw-Hill.

BMVI. (2016). Dobrindt: The way for automated vehicles is clear. Federal Cabinet adopts transposition of Vienna Convention. Retrieved from Federal Ministry of Transport and Digital Infrastructure: https://www.bmvi.de/SharedDocs/EN/PressRelease/2016/044-dobrindt-automated-driving.html.

Bogner, A., Littig, B., & Menz, W. (2009). Interviewing Experts. New York: Palgrave MacMillan.

Bordonali, C., Ferraresi, S., & Richter, W. (2017). Shifting Gear in Cyber Security for Connected Cars. online: McKinsey.

References

Boston, W. (2008). The Time. Retrieved July 16, 2017, from Germany's Car INdustry Crashes: http://content.time.com/time/world/article/0,8599,1849410,00.html.

Brewer, J. (2003). Credo Reference. (SAGE, Editor) Retrieved December 5, 2014, from The A-Z of social research: http://search.credoreference.com.ezproxy.uwe.ac.uk/content/entry/sageuksr/induction/0.

Bryman, A., & Bell, E. (2007). Business Research Methods (2nd Edition ed.). Oxford: Oxford University Press.

Bunghez, C. L. (2015). The Future of Transportation - Autonomous Vehicles. International Journal of Economic Practices and Theories, 5(5), 447-454.

Burnett, S. (2017). Workers look on nervously as Mercedes works on self-building technology. Retrieved July 18, 2017, from Motor 1: https://uk.motor1.com/news/173894/mercedes-sclass-self-driving/.

Carty, S. S. (2017). Failed Google deal left Fields in the lurch. Retrieved October 29, 2017, from Automotive News: http://www.autonews.com/article/20170529/OEM/170529795/google-ford-deal-mark-fields.

CB Insights. (2017). 44 Corporations Working On Autonomous Vehicles. Retrieved October 06, 2017, from CB Insights: https://www.cbinsights.com/research/autonomous-driverless-vehicles-corporations-list/.

Christensen, C. M. (2013). The Innovator's Dilemma: When New Technologies Cause Great Firms to Fail (Management of Innovation and Change). Boston: Harvard Business Review Press.

Collier, J. L. (2006). The Automobile. New York: Cavendish Square Publishing.

Congress of the United States Office of Technology Assessment. (1995). Innovation and Commercialization of Emerging Technologies. Washington, DC: U.S. Government Printing Office.

Crowther, D., & Lancaster, G. (2008). Research Methods: A concise Introduction to Research in Management and Business Consultancy. Oxford: Elsevier.

Czaja, R., & Blair, J. (2005). Designing Surveys: A Guide to Decision and Procedures. Thousand Oaks: Pine Forge Press.

References

Dahlberg, L., & McCaig, C. (2010). Practical Research and Evaluation: A Start-to-Finish Guide for Practitioners. New Delhi: SAGE.

Daimler. (2017). On the way to autonomous driving: Baden-Württemberg is setting the pace for the mobility of tomorrow. Retrieved October 31, 2017, from Daimler: http://media.daimler.com/marsMediaSite/en/instance/ko/On-the-way-to-autonomous-driving-Baden-Wuerttemberg-is-setting-the-pace-for-the-mobility-of-tomorrow.xhtml?oid=29944087.

Daimler AG. (2017). Company History. Retrieved July 15, 2017, from Daimler Group: https://www.daimler.com/company/tradition/company-history/1885-1886.html.

Daimler AG. (n.d). CASE: New Strategic focus for Mercedes-Benz Cars Strategy. Retrieved July 29, 2017, from Innovation: https://www.daimler.com/innovation/specials/electric-mobility/case.html.

Denzin, N., & Lincoln, Y. (2000). Handbook of Qualitative Research. London: SAGE.

DHL. (2014). Self-Driving Vehicles in Logistics. A DHL Perspective on Implications and Use Cases for the Logistics Industry. Troisdorf: DHL Trend Research.

Driscoll, K. R., Roy, A., Ponchak, D. S., & Downey, A. N. (2017). Cyber safety and security for reduced crew operations (RCO). 2017 IEEE/AIAA 36th Digital Avionics Systems Conference (DASC) (pp. 1 - 10). St. Petersburg: IEEE.

Elsevier. (2018). What is peer review? Retrieved February 10, 2018, from Elsevier: https://www.elsevier.com/reviewers/what-is-peer-review.

English, A. (2011). Skoda Celebrates 20 Years of Succes under VW. Retrieved July 16, 2017, from The Telegraph: http://www.telegraph.co.uk/motoring/car-manufacturers/skoda/8458395/Skoda-celebrates-20-years-of-success-under-VW.html.

ENO. (2013). Preparing a Nation for Autonomous Vehicles: Opportunities, Barriers and Policy Recommendations. Washington, DC: ENO Center for Transportation.

References

Federal Minister of Transport and Digital Infrastructure. (2017). Ethics Commission: Automated and Connected Driving. Online: Federal Minister of Transport and Digital Infrastructure. Retrieved October 31, 2017, from https://www.bmvi.de/SharedDocs/EN/Documents/G/ethic-commission-report.pdf?_blob=publicationFile.

Fielding, N., Lee, R. M., & Blank, G. (2008). Online Research Methods. Los Angeles: SAGE.

Finkbeiner, P. (2017). Social Media for Knowledge Sharing in Automotive Repair. Heidelberg: Springer.

Flick, U. (2014). An Introduction to Qualitative Research. Singapore: SAGE.

Flink, J. J. (1990). The Automobile Age. Cambridge: The MIT Press.

Ford Motor Company. (2002). The Ford Century: Ford Motor Company and the Innovations that Shaped the World. New York: Artisan. Retrieved 07 15, 2017, from F: https://corporate.ford.com/history.html.

Ford Motor Company. (2017). Annual Reports. Retrieved October 15, 2017, from Ford Motor Company: http://shareholder.ford.com/financials/annual-reports.

Foster, I., Ghani, R., Jarmin, R. S., Kreuter, F., & Lane, J. (2017). Big Data and Social Science: A Practical Guide to Methods and Tools. New York: CRC Press.

Fourie, L. F. (2016). On a Global Mission: The Automobiles of General Motors International Volume 3: GM Worldwide Review, North American Specifications and Executives Listings. Toronto: Friesenpress.

Freyssenet, M. (2009). The Second Automobile Revolution. Trajectories of the World Carmakers in the XXI Century. New York: Palgrave MacMillan.

Friar, J. H., & Balachandra, R. (2016). Spotting the Customer for Emerging Technologies. Research-Technology Management, 42(4), 37-43.

Fujimoto, T. (1999). The Evolution of A Manufacturing System at Toyota. Oxford: Oxford University Press.

Given, L. M. (2008). The SAGE Encyclopedia of Qualitative Research Methods (Vol. 2). Los Angeles: SAGE.

Goodwin, W. L., & Goodwin, L. D. (1996). Understanding Quantitative and Qualitative Research in Early Childhood Education. New York: Teachers College.

References

Grosse-Ophoff, A., Hausler, S., Heineke, K., & Möller, T. (2017). How shared mobility will change the automotive industry. Retrieved December 29, 2017, from McKinsey: https://www.mckinsey.com/industries/automotive-and-assembly/our-insights/how-shared-mobility-will-change-the-automotive-industry.

GTAI. (2017). Automotive Industry: Germany – The World's Automotive Hub of Innovation. Retrieved December 29, 2017, from Germany Trade & Invest: http://www.gtai.de/GTAI/Navigation/EN/Invest/Industries/Mobility/automotive.html.

Hair, J. F., Wolfinbarger, M., Money, A. H., Samouel, P., & Page, M. J. (2011). Essentials of Business Research Methods (2nd ed.). London: M.E. Sharpe.

Halperin, S., & Heath, O. (2017). Political Research: Methods and Practical Skills. Oxford: Oxford University Press.

Hanley, S. (2018). GM Leads, Tesla & Apple Trail Deeply In Navigant Research Self-Driving Report. CleanTechnica. Retrieved January 20, 2018, from https://cleantechnica.com/2018/01/20/gm-leads-tesla-apple-trail-deeply-navigant-research-self-driving-report/.

Heineke, K., Möller, T., Padhi, A., & Tschiesner, A. (2017). The Automotive Revolution is Speeding Up. Retrieved December 29, 2017, from McKinsey: https://www.mckinsey.com/industries/automotive-and-assembly/our-insights/the-automotive-revolution-is-speeding-up.

Heneric, O., Licht, G., & Sofka, W. (2005). Europe's Automotive Industry on the Move: Competitiveness in a Changing World. Heidelberg: ZEW.

Hess, T. M. (1990). Aging and Cognition: Knowledge Organization and Utilization. Amsterdam: North Holland.

Hirsh, E., Hedlund, S., & Schweizer, M. (2003). Reality Is Perception: The Truth about Car Brands. Fall 2003(32). Retrieved July 16, 2017, from Strategy + Business: https://www.strategy-business.com/article/03302?gko=fbb50.

IFO Institute for Economic Research & Shuka Institute of Research. (1997). A Comparative Analysis of Japanese and German Economic Success. Heidelberg: Springer.

Information Resources Management Association USA. (2017). Media Influence: Breakthroughs in Research Practice. Hershey: IGI Global.

References

International Transport Forum. (2015). Automated and Autonomous Driving: Regulation under Uncertainty. Online: OECD. Retrieved from https://www.itf-oecd.org/sites/default/files/docs/15cpb_autonomousdriving.pdf.

Isaac, M. (2017). Lyft Adds Ford to Its List of Self-Driving Car Partners. Retrieved October 29, 2017, from The New York Times: https://www.nytimes.com/2017/09/27/technology/lyft-ford-self-driving-cars.html.

Isaac, M., & Boudette, N. E. (2016). Automakers Befriend Start-Ups Like Uber, Girding Against a Changing Car Culture. Retrieved August 26, 2017, from The New York Times: https://www.nytimes.com/2016/05/25/technology/uber-gett-ridesharing-toyota-vw.html?mcubz=3.

Jahankhani, H., Carlile, A., Emm, D., Hosseinian-Far, A., Brown, G., Sexton, G., & Jamal, A. (2017). Global Security, Safety and Sustainability. The Security Challenges of the Connected World. 11th International Conference, ICGS3 (pp. 308-393). New York: Springer.

Janasz, T. (2016). Paradigm Shift in Urban Mobility. Towards Factor 10 of Automobility. Heidelberg: Springer.

Jawadekar, W. S. (2011). Knowledge Managemen. New Delhi: Tata McGraw Hill Education.

Joosten, T. (2012). Social Media For Educators: Strategies and Best Practices. New York: Jossey-Bass.

Joseph, U. A. (2013). The 'Made in Germany' Champion Brands: Nation Branding, Innovation and World Export Leadership. London: Routledge.

Katsirikou, A., & Skiadas, C. (2012). New Trends in Qualitative and Quantitative Methods in Libraries. London: World Scientific.

Keay, A. (2011). The Corporate Objective. Cheltenham: Edward Elgar.

Kirsh, S. J. (2010). Media and Youth: A Developmental Perspective. London: Wiley.

Klenke, K. (2016). Qualitative Research in the Study of Leadership. London: Emerald Group.

References

Kollewe, J. (2012). Germany enjoys strongest economic growth since reunification. Retrieved July 16, 2017, from The Guardian: https://www.theguardian.com/world/2011/jan/12/germany-enjoys-economic-growth-spurt.

Konthari, C. R. (2004). Research Methodology: Methods and Techniques (2nd ed.). Ranchi: New Age.

Korosec, K. (2016). Meet the Future Buyers of Self-Driving Cars. Retrieved August 21, 2017, from Fortune: The 21st Century Corporation: http://fortune.com/2016/04/22/self-driving-cars-poll/.

Kudo, A., Kipping, M., & Schröter, H. G. (2004). German and Japanese Business in the Boom Years: Transforming American Management and Technology Models. London: Routledge.

Kumar, R. (2011). Research Methodology: A Step-by-Step Guide for Beginners (3rd ed.). Los Angeles: SAGE.

Kuper, S. (2016). Driverless cars will change everything. Retrieved October 06, 2017, from Financial Times: https://www.ft.com/content/042a04f0-958c-11e6-a80e-bcd69f323a8b?mhq5j=e5.

Kvale, S., & Brinkmann, S. (2009). Interviews: Learning the Craft of Qualitative Research Interviewing (2nd ed.). London: SAGE.

La Monica, P. R. (2015). Volkswagen has plunged 50%. Will it ever recover? Retrieved December 29, 2017, from CNN Money: http://money.cnn.com/2015/09/24/investing/volkswagen-vw-emissions-scandal-stock/index.html.

Lang, N., Rüßmann, M., Mei-Pochtler, A., Dauner, T., Komiya, S., Mosquet, X., & Dourbara, X. (2016). Self-Driving Vehicles, Robo-Taxis, and the Urban Mobility Revolution. Online: BCG. Retrieved October 24, 2017, from http://www.auto-mat.ch/wAssets/docs/BCG-Self-Driving-Vehicles-Robo-Taxis-and-the-Urban-Mobility-Revolution.pdf.

Laws, S., Harper, C., & Marcus, R. (2003). Research for Development: A Practical Guide. Thousand Oaks: SAGE.

Lepage, J.-D. G. (2007). German Military Vehicles of World War II: An Illustrated Guide to Cars, Trucks, Half-Tracks, Motorcycles, Amphibious Vehicles and Others. Jefferson: McFarland & Company.

References

Lewis, D., & Zitzlsperger, U. (2016). Historical Dictionary of Contemporary Germany (2nd ed.). Toronto: Rowman & Littlefield.

Lewis-Beck, M. S., Bryman, A., & Liao, T. F. (2004). The SAGE Encyclopedia of Social Science Research Methods. Thousand Oaks: SAGE.

Liamputtong, P. (2011). Focus Group Methodology: Principles and Practice. Los Angeles: SAGE.

Lipson, H., & Kurman, M. (2016). Driverless: Intelligent Cars and the Road Ahead. Cambridge: The MIT Press.

Lipson, H., & Kurman, M. (2016). Intelligent Cars and the Road Ahead. Cambridge: The MIT Press.

Mark, R. (2017). The benefits of autonomous technology. Logistics & Transport Focus, 19(2), 24-25.

Marsden, P. V., & Wright, J. D. (2010). Handbook of Survey Research (2nd ed.). London: Emerald.

Martinez-Mesa, J., Gonzáles-Chica, D. A., Duquia, R. P., Donamigo, R. R., & Bastos, J. L. (2016). Sampling: How to Select Participants in my Research Study? An Bras Dermatol, 91(3), 326-330.

Mason, J. (2013). Qualitative Research (2nd Edition ed.). Los Angeles: SAGE.

Maurer, M., Gerdes, C. J., Lenz, B., & Winner, H. (2016). Autonomous Driving: Technical, Legal and Social Aspects. Heidelberg: Springer.

Maxton, G. P., & Wormald, J. (2004). Time for a Model Change: Re-engineering the Global Automotive Industry. Cambridge: Cambridge University Press.

Mayoh, B. (1991). Scandinavian Conference on Artificial Intelligence - 91. Proceedings of the SCAI '91 (pp. 1-345). Roskilde: IOS.

McGuinness, D. (2015). VW scandal threatens 'Made in Germany' brand. Retrieved December 29, 2017, from BBC: http://www.bbc.com/news/world-europe-34328689.

McKinsey. (2014). What's driving the connected car. Retrieved December 29, 2017, from McKinsey: https://www.mckinsey.com/industries/automotive-and-assembly/our-insights/whats-driving-the-connected-car.

References

McKinsey. (2016). Automotive Revolution- Perspective Towards 2030. online: McKinsey. Retrieved July 29, 2017, from McKinsey: https://www.mckinsey.de/files/automotive_revolution_perspective_towards_2030.pdf.

McKinsey. (2016). Car Data: Paving the way to value-creating Mobility Perspectives on a new Automotive Business Model. online: McKinsey. Retrieved from McKinsey: https://www.mckinsey.de/files/mckinsey_car_data_march_2016.pdf.

McNeese, T. (2000). Industrialization and Colonization: The Age of Progress. New York: Lorenz Educational Press.

Meyer, G., & Beiker, S. (2014). Road Vehicle Automation. Heidelberg: Springer.

Meyer, M. A., & Booker, J. M. (2001). Eliciting and Analyzing Expert Judgment. London: SIAM.

Morgan Standley. (2016). Shared Mobility on the Road of the Future. Retrieved December 29, 2017, from Morgan Standley: https://www.morganstanley.com/ideas/car-of-future-is-autonomous-electric-shared-mobility.

Morris, D. Z. (2016). Mercedes-Benz's Self-Driving Cars Would Choose Passenger Lives Over Bystanders. Retrieved October 22, 2017, from Fortune: http://fortune.com/2016/10/15/mercedes-self-driving-car-ethics/.

Mosquet, X., Dauner, T., Lang, N., Rüßmann, M., Mei-Pochtler, A., Agrawal, R., & Schmieg, F. (2015). Revolution in the Driver's Seat: The Road to Autonomous Vehicles. Retrieved November 05, 2017, from BCG: https://www.bcgperspectives.com/content/articles/automotive-consumer-insight-revolution-drivers-seat-road-autonomous-vehicles/.

Mullin, D. (2010). The Failing Logic of Money. London: O-Books.

National Conference of State Legislatures. (2018). Autonomous Vehicles | Self-Driving Vehicles Enacted Legislation. Retrieved November 01, 2017, from National Conference of State Legislatures: http://www.ncsl.org/research/transportation/autonomous-vehicles-self-driving-vehicles-enacted-legislation.aspx.

NHTSA. (2013). U.S. Department of Transportation Releases Policy on Automated Vehicle Development. Retrieved July 17, 2017, from U.S. Department of Transportation: https://www.transportation.gov/briefing-room/us-department-transportation-releases-policy-automated-vehicle-development.

Norton Rose Fulbright. (2016). Autonomous vehicles: The Legal Landscape in the US and Germany. Online: Norton Rose Fulbright. Retrieved October 31, 2017, from http://www.nortonrosefulbright.com/files/20160726-autonomous-vehicles-the-legal-landscape-in-the-us-and-germany-141559.pdf.

Norton Rose Fulbright. (2017). Autonomous Vehicles: The Legal Landscape of Dedicated Short Range Communication in the US, UK and Germany. Online: Norton Rose Fulbright. Retrieved October 31, 2017, from http://www.nortonrosefulbright.com/files/20170712-autonomous-vehicles-the-legal-landscape-of-dedicated-short-range-communication-in-the-us-uk-and-germany-154724.pdf.

Oakshott, L. (2012). Essential Quantitative Methods (5th Edition ed.). Hampshire: Palgrave McMillan.

Omohundro, S. (2014). Autonomous technology and the greater human good. Journal of Experimental & Theoretical Artificial Intelligence, 26(3), 303-315.

Overly, S. (2017). The big moral dilemma facing self-driving cars. Retrieved October 22, 2017, from The Washington Post: https://www.washingtonpost.com/news/innovations/wp/2017/02/20/the-big-moral-dilemma-facing-self-driving-cars/?utm_term=.e183d0e0f42c.

Ozimek, A. (2014). The Massive Economic Benefits Of Self-Driving Cars. Retrieved October 06, 2017, from Forbes: https://www.forbes.com/sites/modeledbehavior/2014/11/08/the-massive-economic-benefits-of-self-driving-cars/#44de66d83273.

Parissien, S. (2013). The Life of the Automobile: A New History of the Motor Car. London: Atlantic Books.

Parment, A. (2014). Auto Brand: Building Successful Car Brands for the Future. Philadelphia: Kogan Page.

Pathak, N. (2017). Artificial Intelligence for .NET: Speech, Language and Search. Building Smart Applications with Microsoft Cognitive Services APIs. New Delhi: Apress.

Peterson, G. (2016). Consumer Interest In Self-Driving Cars Increasing. Retrieved November 05, 2017, from Forbes: https://www.forbes.com/sites/georgepeterson1/2016/06/05/consumer-interest-in-self-driving-cars-increasing/#7c3bc4a11011.

Pfeffermann, D., & Rao, C. R. (2009). Sample Surveys: Design, Methods and Application (Vol. 29A). Paris: Elsevier.

Ploeg, J. (2017). Cooperative Vehicle Automation: Safety Aspects and Control Software Architecture. 2017 IEEE International Conference on Software Architecture Workshops (ICSAW) (p. 6). Gothenburg, Sweden: IEEE.

Pohl, H., & Rudolph, B. (1990). German Yearbook on Business History 1988. Heidelberg: Springer-Verlag.

Preissl, B., & Solimene, L. (2003). The Dynamics of Clusters and Innovation: Beyond Systems and Networks. Heidelberg: Springer.

Punch, K. F. (2016). Developing Effective Research Proposals. Los Angeles: SAGE.

Putre, L. (2016). Automakers are Gearing up for Self-Driving Cars, But Is Anyone Else? Retrieved November 05, 2017, from IndustryWeek: http://www.industryweek.com/emerging-technologies/automakers-are-gearing-self-driving-cars-anyone-else.

Quinlan, C. (2011). Business Research Methods. Hampshire, UK: Cengage Learning.

Regan, M. A., Horberry, T., & Stevens, A. (2014). Driver Acceptance of New Technology. Theory, Measurement and Optimisation. London: Ashgate.

Roberts, K. J. (2005). Brand Challenges and UNderstanding the Brand Core. In B. Gottschalk, R. Kalmbach, & J. Dannenberg, Markenmanagement in der Automobilindustrie: DIe Erfolgsstrategien (pp. 101-122). Heidelberg: Gabler.

Rogers, E. M. (2010). Diffusion of Innovations (4th Edition ed.). New York: The Free Press.

References

Roland Berger. (2014). Autonomous Driving: Disruptive innovation that promises to change the automotive industry as we know it — it's time for every player to think:act! Think Act.

Rosenzweig, J., & Bartl, M. (2015). A Review and Analysis of Literature on Autonomous Driving. The Making-Of Innovation, E-Journal, 1-57.

SAE International. (2014). SAE J3016: Taxonomy and Definitions for Terms Related to Driving Automation Systems for On-Road Motor Vehicles. n.a: SAE International. Retrieved from SAE International.

Salkind, N. J. (2010). Encyclopedia of Research Design. Los Angeles: SAGE.

Saunders, M., Lewis, P., & Thornhill, A. (2012). Research Methods for Business Students. Essex: Pearson Education.

Savic, V., Schiller, E. M., & Papatriantafilou, M. (2017). Distributed algorithm for collision avoidance at road intersections in the presence of communication failures. 2017 IEEE Intelligent Vehicles Symposium (IV) (pp. 1005 - 1012). Los Angeles: IEEE.

Schoettle, B., & Sivak, M. (2014). A Survey of Public Opinion about Autonomous and Self-Driving Vehicles in the U.S., the U.K., and Australia. University of Michigan Transportation Research Institute, 21, 1-38.

Shepardson, D. (2017). U.S. House unanimously approves sweeping self-driving car measure. Retrieved October 26, 2017, from Reuters: https://www.reuters.com/article/us-autos-selfdriving/u-s-house-unanimously-approves-sweeping-self-driving-car-measure-idUSKCN1BH2B2.

Siciliano, B., & Khatib, O. (2016). Springer Handbook of Robotics. Heidelberg: Springer.

Sinclair, J. L. (2004). The Automobile. New York: Capstone Press.

Smale, A. (2015). In Germany, a Cozy Relationship Between Carmakers and Government. Retrieved August 25, 2017, from The New York Times: https://www.nytimes.com/2015/10/02/world/europe/germany-volkswagen-autos-merkel.html?mcubz=3.

Smith, N. C., & Dainty, P. (1991). The management research handbook. London: Routledge.

References

Sreejesh, S., Mohapatra, S., & Anusree, M. R. (2014). Business Research Methods: An Applied Orientation. Heidelberg: Springer.

Taylor, B., Sinha, G., & Ghoshal, T. (2006). Research Methodology: A Guide for Researchers in Management and Social Sciences. New Delhi: Prentice-Hall of India.

Taylor, E., & Potter, M. (2017). Timeline: Volkswagen's long road to a U.S. Dieselgate settlement. Retrieved July 16, 2017, from Reuters: http://www.reuters.com/article/us-volkswagen-emissions-timeline-idUSKBN14V100.

Taylor, M. (2017). The Level 3 Audi A8 Will Almost Be The Most Important Car In The World. Retrieved September 15, 2017, from Forbes: https://www.forbes.com/sites/michaeltaylor/2017/09/10/tthe-level-3-audi-a8-will-almost-be-the-most-important-car-in-the-world/#4f9638dbfb3d

The Economist. (2017). Why carmakers need to get bigger. Retrieved August 26, 2017, from The Economist: https://www.economist.com/news/business/21720658-gms-recent-sale-opel-has-revived-talk-mega-mergers-why-carmakers-need-get-bigger.

Times, F. (2017). Electrified vehicles to take half of global auto market by 2030. Retrieved December 29, 2017, from Financial Times: http://www.ft.lk/opinion/Electrified-vehicles-to-take-half-of-global-auto-market-by-2030/14-645054.

Toews, R. (2017). The AI Debate Critical to the Future of Autonomous Vehicles. Retrieved October 22, 2017, from Forbes: https://www.forbes.com/sites/currentaccounts/2017/03/09/the-ai-debate-critical-to-the-future-of-autonomous-vehicles/2/#778a6030499c.

Topham, G. (2012). Volkswagen Swallows Porsche. Retrieved July 16, 2017, from The Guardian: https://www.theguardian.com/business/2012/jul/05/volkswagen-buys-porsche.

Toyota Motor Corporation. (2017). Annual Report. Retrieved October 15, 2017, from Toyota Motor Corporation: http://www.toyota-global.com/investors/ir_library/annual/back/.

References

Tryfonas, T. (2016). Human Aspects of Information Security, Privacy, and Trust. 4th International Conference, Held as Part of HCI International 2016 (pp. 1-287). Heidelberg: Springer.

U.S. Department of Transportation. (n.d.). Table 1-23: World Motor Vehicle Production, Selected Countries (Thousands of vehicles). Retrieved July 16, 2017, from Bureau of Transportation Statistics: https://www.rita.dot.gov/bts/sites/rita.dot.gov.bts/files/publications/national_transportation_statistics/html/table_01_23.html_mfd.

United States Department of Transportation. (n.d.). Communication. DSRC: The Future of Safer Driving. Retrieved October 20, 2017, from Intelligent Transportation Systems. Joint Program Office: https://www.its.dot.gov/factsheets/dsrc_factsheet.htm.

VDA. (2016). Automobile Production: Figures on national and international automobile production. Retrieved July 17, 2017, from Verband der Automobilindustrie e.V.: https://www.vda.de/en/services/facts-and-figures/annual-figures/automobile-production.html.

VDA. (2017). Mobility of Tomorrow Initiative: "Changes are not a threat, but an opportunity". Retrieved from Mobility of Tomorrow Initiative: https://www.mobilitaet-von-morgen.de/6-dialog-en/changes-are-not-a-threat-but-an-opportunity?lang=en.

Volkswagen AG. (2017). Annual Reports. Retrieved October 15, 2017, from Volkswagen AG: https://www.volkswagenag.com/en/InvestorRelations/news-and-publications/Annual_Reports.html.

Wacket, M., Escritt, T., & Davis, T. (2017). Germany adopts self-driving vehicles law. Retrieved October 31, 2017, from Reuters: https://www.reuters.com/article/us-germany-autos-self-driving/germany-adopts-self-driving-vehicles-law-idUSKBN1881HY.

Warner, R. M. (2013). Applied Statistics: From Bivariate Through Multivariate Techniques (2nd ed.). Singapore: SAGE.

Weeks, L. H. (2010). The History of the Automobile and its Inventors. Bremen: Europaeischer Hochschulverlag.

Weeks, L. H. (2011). Origin and Development of the Automobile. Bremen: Europaeischer Hochschulverlag.

Wengraf, T. (2001). Qualitative Research Interviewing. London: SAGE.

Wilson, J. R., & Sharples, S. (2015). Evaluation of Human Work. Boca Raton: CRC Press.

Wladawsky-Berger, I. (2016). The Evolving Automotive Ecosystem. Retrieved December 29, 2017, from The Wall Street Journal: https://blogs.wsj.com/cio/2015/04/06/the-evolving-automotive-ecosystem/.

Zolait, A. H. (2013). Technology Diffusion and Adoption: Global Complexity, Global Innovation. New York: ICI Global.

Appendices

Appendix A: VW vs. main Competitors: Units Sold in 2004 and 2014

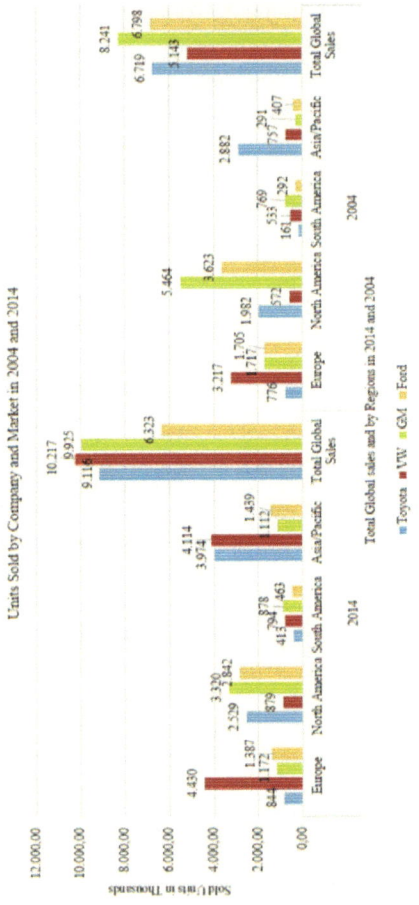

Appendix A. Data adopted from Volkswagen AG. (2017). Annual Reports. Retrieved October 15, 2017, from Volkswagen AG:
https://www.volkswagenag.com/en/InvestorRelations/news-and-publications/Annual_Reports.html, Ford Motor Company. (2017). Annual Reports. Retrieved October 15, 2017, from Ford Motor Company:
http://shareholder.ford.com/financials/annual-reports, Toyota Motor Corporation. (2017). Annual Report. Retrieved October 15, 2017, from Toyota Motor Corporation: http://www.toyota-global.com/investors/ir_library/annual/back/ , & AnnualReports.com. (2017). Annual Reports. Retrieved October 15, 2017, from General Anhang 2

Appendix B: SAE International Levels of Autonomous Driving

SAE Level	Name	Narrative Definition	Execution of Steering and Acceleration/Deceleration	Monitoring of driving Environment	Fallback Performance of Dynamic Task	System Capability (Driving Modes)
		Human driver monitors the driving environment				
0	No Automation	the full-time performance by the human driver of all aspects of the dynamic driving task, even when enhanced by warning or intervention systems	Human Driver	Human Driver	Human Driver	n/a
1	Driver Assistance	the driving mode-specific execution by a driver assistance system of either steering or acceleration/deceleration using information about the driving environment and with the expectation that the human driver perform all remaining aspects of the dynamic driving task	Human Driver and System	Human Driver	Human Driver	Some driving modes
2	Partial Automation	the driving mode-specific execution by one or more driver assistance systems of both steering and acceleration/deceleration using information about the driving environment and with the expectation that the human driver perform all remaining aspects of the dynamic driving task	System	Human Driver	Human Driver	Some driving modes
		Automated driving system monitors the driving environment				
3	Conditional Automation	the driving mode-specific performance by an automated driving system of all aspects of the dynamic driving task with the expectation that the human driver will respond appropriately to a request to intervene	System	System	Human Driver	Some driving modes
4	High Automation	the driving mode-specific performance by an automated driving system of all aspects of the dynamic driving task, even if a human driver does not respond appropriately to a request to intervene	System	System	System	Some driving modes
5	Full Automation	the full-time performance by an automated driving system of all aspects of the dynamic driving task under all roadway and environmental conditions that can be managed by a human driver	System	System	System	All driving modes

Appendix B. Adopted from SAE International. (2014). SAE J3016: Taxonomy and Definitions for Terms Related to Driving Automation Systems for On-Road Motor Vehicles. n.a: SAE International. Retrieved from SAE International.

Appendix C: GM Leads, Tesla & Apple Trail Deeply In Navigant Research Self-Driving Report

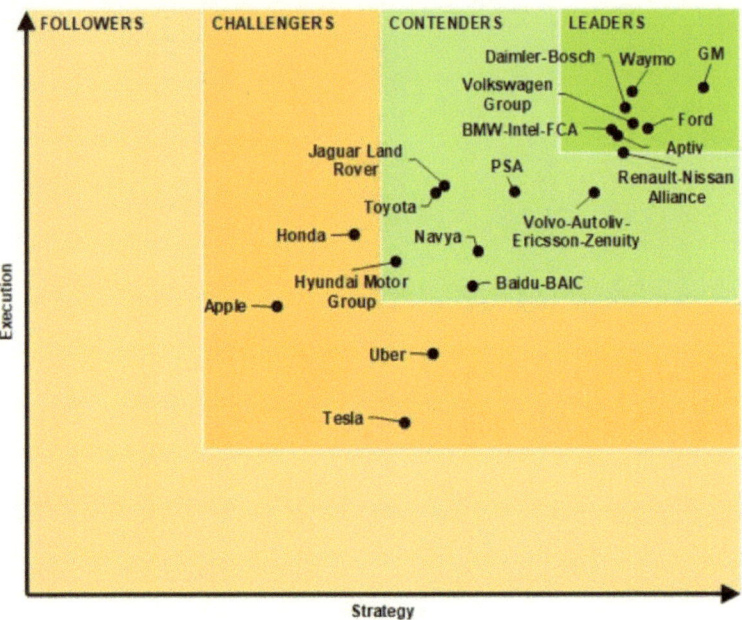

Appendix C. Adopted from Hanley, S. (2018). GM Leads, Tesla & Apple Trail Deeply In Navigant Research Self-Driving Report. CleanTechnica. Retrieved January 20, 2018, from https://cleantechnica.com/2018/01/20/gm-leads-tesla-apple-trail-deeply-navigant-research-self-driving-report/.

Appendices

Appendix D: US States with Enacted Autonomous Vehicle Legislation

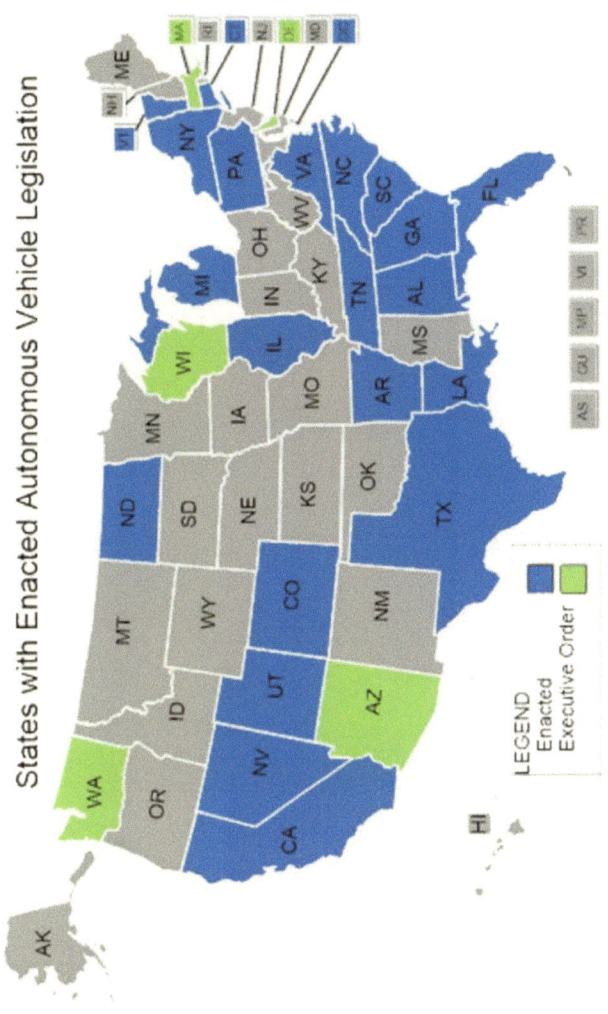

Appendix D. Adopted from National Conference of State Legislatures. (2018). Autonomous Vehicles | Self-Driving Vehicles Enacted Legislation. Retrieved November 01, 2017, from National Conference of State Legislatures:
http://www.ncsl.org/research/transportation/autonomous-vehicles-self-driving-vehicles-enacted-legislation.aspx

Appendix E: Rogers Product Adoption Curve

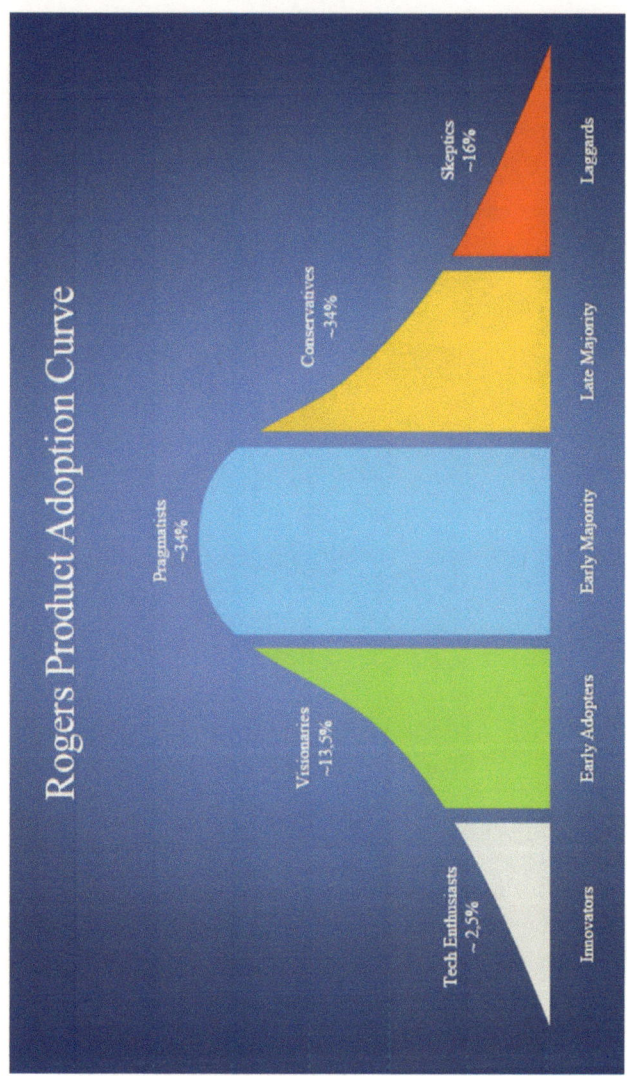

Appendix E. Adapted from Rogers, E. M. (2010). Diffusion of Innovations (4th Edition ed.). New York: The Free Press

Appendix F: Survey on Customer Readiness

Autonomous Driving

GENERAL INFORMATION

First of all, thank you very much for your participation in advance!

I would like to invite you to take part in a research study exploring the status quo and the major obstacles of the German car manufacturing industry with respect to autonomous driving. Prior to your participation, please take some time to read through the following information carefully in order to understand the purpose and the aim of the research as well as what is required of you. Furthermore, please do not hesitate to ask questions if anything you read is not clear or if you would like more information. Take time to decide whether you would like to participate.

Why have I been invited?
You have been invited to participate in the survey based on your nationality and age.

Do I have to take part?
No, the decision is yours to make. Please read the following information carefully. By participating in the survey you allow the researcher to use the information of your inserted answers. You are free to withdraw at any time, without giving a reason.

What will I have to do if I take part?
In case you accept the invitation and take part in the research project, you will have to participate in a survey and answer a few questions. The survey will last approximately 10 minutes. It is expected that you answer the questions honestly and in your best effort. No further participation is required.

Will my participation in the study be kept confidential?
All information which is collected about you will be kept strictly confidential. Within the research project your name will never appear and thus your answers will be anonymous. A master list, containing participants' codes as well as data will be held on a password protected computer accessed only the researcher. Your answers will be collected through the survey platform and will be extracted for further analysis.

What will happen to the results of the research study?
The use of the results are incumbent upon the researcher. If requested, I will send you a copy of the final report as soon as it is finished.

Further information and contact details:
- Jan KACHELMAIER – jan.kachelmaier@grenoble-em.com

*Required

1.
How willing are you to use autonomous vehicles? *
Mark only one oval.

	1	2	3	4	5	
not at all	○	○	○	○	○	absolutely

Appendices

2. Are you willing to give up your car to use only autonomous vehicles of mobility providers (assuming mobility coverage is sufficient)? *
Mark only one oval.

◯ Yes
◯ No
◯ Maybe

3. Considering your daily mobility, how important are the following criteria? *
Mark only one oval per row.

	1 (not important at all)	2	3 (neither...nor)	4	5 (of utmost importance)
Safety	◯	◯	◯	◯	◯
Independence	◯	◯	◯	◯	◯
Stress avoidance	◯	◯	◯	◯	◯
Freedom during the ride (ability to read, work, relax, etc.)	◯	◯	◯	◯	◯
Cost	◯	◯	◯	◯	◯
Time	◯	◯	◯	◯	◯
Comfort	◯	◯	◯	◯	◯
Convenience	◯	◯	◯	◯	◯
Social status	◯	◯	◯	◯	◯
Driving experience/fun	◯	◯	◯	◯	◯

4. Would you be concerned to ride in an autonomous vehicle without any steering wheel and pedals? *
Mark only one oval.

◯ Yes
◯ No

5. Would you prefer to ride in a conventional vehicle with full AD-ability that you can switch on and off whenever you like, or do you prefere a specially designed autonomous vehicle? *
Mark only one oval.

◯ Conventional vehicle
◯ Specially designed autonomous vehicles
◯ It does not matter to me

6. **How safe do you consider autonomous vehicles for passenger? (3= as safe as current non-autonomous vehicles)** *

   Mark only one oval.

	1	2	3	4	5	
not safe at all	○	○	○	○	○	absolutely safe

7. **How safe do you consider autonomous vehicles to be for pedestrians (walking around on the streets)? (3=as safe as current non-autonomous vehicles)** *

   Mark only one oval.

	1	2	3	4	5	
not safe at all	○	○	○	○	○	absolutely safe

8. **Do you rather trust a traditional car manufacturer (e.g. Daimler or BMW) or would you consider newcomers (e.g. Apple or Google) to be more trustworthy?** *

   Mark only one oval.

   ○ Traditional car manufacturers (e.g. Daimler, BMW or VW)
   ○ New autonomous vehicle providers (e.g. Google, Apple)
   ○ I trust both equally

9. **Are you afraid of any cyberattacks on autonomous vehicles?** *

   Mark only one oval.

   ○ Yes
   ○ No
   ○ I do not know

10. **How much would you be influenced in your opinion on autonomous vehicles by positive newspaper articles (e.g. no accident in the last year)?** *

    Mark only one oval.

	1	2	3	4	5	
not at all	○	○	○	○	○	changes my mind completely

11. **How much would you be influenced in your opinion on autonomous vehicles by negative newspaper articles (e.g. another horror crash in an autonomous vehicle, several people dead)?** *

    Mark only one oval.

	1	2	3	4	5	
not at all	○	○	○	○	○	changes my mind completely

12. **How would you rate your overall knowledge of autonomous vehicles, including advantages and disadvantages?** *

    Mark only one oval.

	1	2	3	4	5	
no knowledge at all	○	○	○	○	○	know everything

Personal Information

13. **What area are you living in?** *

    Mark only one oval.

    ○ Urban/city

    ○ Rural

14. **What is your age?** *

    _____

Appendix G: Age Distribution of Survey Respondents

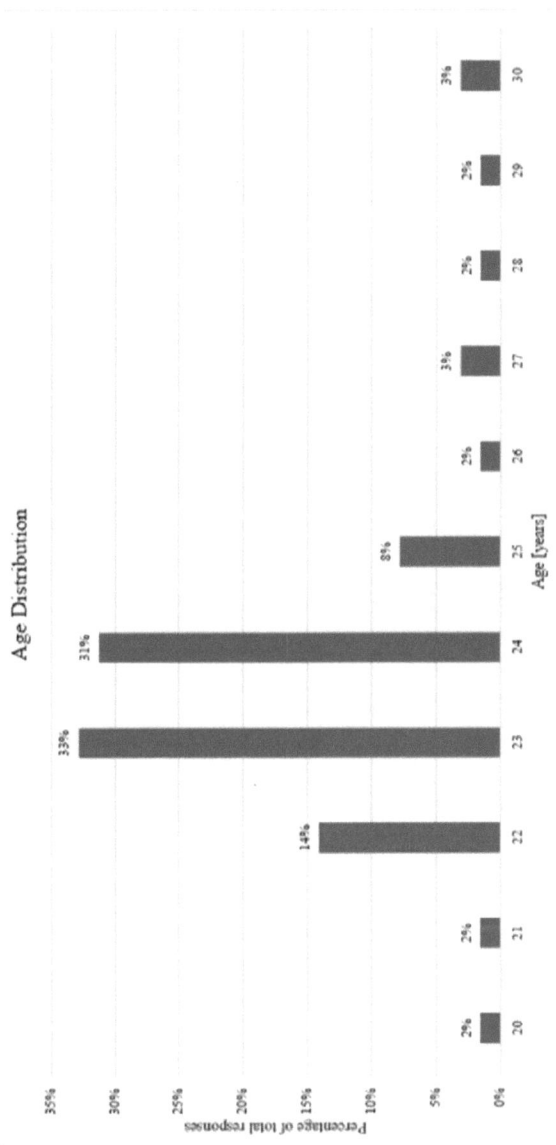

Appendix G. Excel histogram of respondents' age distribution.

Appendix H: T-test on Willingness to use AVs by Gender

t-Test: Two-Sample Assuming Equal Variances		
	male	female
Mean	3,59375	3,0625
Variance	1,28125	1,28629032
Observations	32	32
Pooled Variance	1,28377016	
Hypothesized Mean Difference	0	
df	62	
t Stat	1,87549234	
P(T<=t) one-tail	0,0327178	
t Critical one-tail	1,66980416	
P(T<=t) two-tail	0,0654356	
t Critical two-tail	1,99897152	

Appendix H. Output of Excel t-test analysis.

Appendix I: ANOVA on Willingness to give up One's own Car and Importance of Driving Experience for Female Participants.

ANOVA						
ource of Variation	SS	df	MS	F	P-value	F crit
Between Groups	0,59375	2	0,296875	0,186653	0,83072043	3,327654499
Within Groups	46,125	29	1,590517241			
Total	46,71875	31				

Appendix I. Output of Excel Anova analysis.

Appendix J: T-test on Influence of Positive and Negative News of AVs on males

t-Test: Two-Sample Assuming Equal Variances		
	How much would you be influenced in your opinion on autonomous vehicles by positive newspaper articles (e.g. no accident in the last year)?	How much would you be influenced in your opinion on autonomous vehicles by negative newspaper articles (e.g. another horror crash in an autonomous vehicle, several people dead)?
Mean	2,59375	2,96875
Variance	1,087701613	1,321572581
Observations	32	32
Pooled Variance	1,204637097	
Hypothesized Mean Difference	0	
df	62	
t Stat	-1,366668368	
P(T<=t) one-tail	0,0883325	
t Critical one-tail	1,669804163	
P(T<=t) two-tail	0,176665	
t Critical two-tail	1,998971517	

Appendix J. Output of Excel t-test analysis